HELLS HEROES

How an unlikely alliance saved Idaho's Hells Canyon

Chris Carlson

To the late Ken Robison who gave a full lifetime of extraordinary service to protecting the many special places in his beloved Idaho. And to Rick Richards who hiked many a mile many times through Hells Canyon with me.

Hells Heroes
ISBN# 978-087004-623-0
© 2018 by Chris Carlson

All rights reserved. No part of this book may be reproduced in any manner without the express written consent of the publisher, except in the case of brief excerpts in critical reviews and articles. All inquiries should be addressed to: Caxton Press, 312 Main Street, Caldwell, ID 83605.

First Edition

LC record available at http://lccn.loc.gov/2018934734
Library of Congress Control Number: 2018934734

Cover and book design by Jocelyn Robertson

Printed in the United States of America
CAXTON PRESS
Caldwell, Idaho
200732

TABLE OF CONTENTS

Forward *Rick Johnson*   1
Introduction   5
Overview   15

The Early Days   39
The Committee of Nine, Idaho Power
& Len B. Jordan   51
Game-changers: Gracie Pfost
& Bill Hamilton   65
The Hells Canyon Preservation Council   73
Brock Evans to the Rescue   87
Frank Church, LBJ & the Politics of Hell   103
Just Around the Bend   113
The Hells Canyon NRA Act of 1975   129
Sandra Mitchell & the Hells Canyon Alliance   135
Legislation: Facts to Justify Regs   147
The Future of Almost Heaven   175

Appendix
    Responsible Shared Use *Sandra Mitchell* 185
    The Heroes of Hells Canyon   191
    Acknowledgments   193
    Bibliography   197
    Public Law 94-199   201
    Timeline   205

FOREWORD

~ *Rick Johnson*
Executive Director of the Idaho Conservation League

THE WINDING TRAIL I've traveled in conservation began with special places. Discovering places that speak to you is a gift. Be it a special view, the cry of an eagle, perhaps the pull of a cutthroat trout on a fly line, these experiences become memories that shape who we are. The pull of a landscape only grows when you begin taking actions to steward and protect these places that become special to you.

Photo: Idaho Conservation League

While special places drew me into this work, special people keep me in it. These include remarkable leaders like the late Governor Cecil D. Andrus and Representative Mike Simpson, but no less, are extraordinary people who've shared time, lessons, and most importantly, their spirit and passion. Some of these people were colleagues and mentors. More than a few started as opponents, but even here a shared passion for place creates remarkable connections.

Much of this book rests, appropriately, on the shoulders of Brock Evans. Brock was an early mentor of mine, and the very first speaker at a conference I helped establish at Idaho's Redfish Lake in the 1980s. I was a fresh-faced staffer for the Idaho Conservation League and Brock already had a near-mythical reputation as a conservationist. Like countless others before and after, I listened to the stories of campaigns won and lost, years of experience he could distill into his mantra of "Endless pressure, endlessly applied." Few lessons have served me so well, and for Brock, Hells Canyon is one of the places he learned it.

I would later work with Brock, quite closely, in and out of Washington, D.C., as part of a remarkable coalition working to preserve the ancient forests of the Pacific Northwest. Working for the Sierra Club in the office Brock once staffed in Seattle, my sense of the region, its people, and the landscapes that shape the Northwest became more fully formed. Those experiences, including time with Brock, have grounded me in my decades back in Idaho.

Sandra Mitchell, also appropriately, plays an important role in these pages. A timber executive once said to me, "We've been fighting so long we've become friends." That's true for Sandra, too. She's a skilled and tenacious advocate, and it's Hells Canyon where she linked place with politics, shaping a career. Through her I have met other great people and better understood the Idaho we call home. And yes, we've become friends.

To start, it doesn't take much to get into conservation work. Passion is your entry fee. But if you're going to pursue this work over the long haul, to make a difference rather than just make a point, you have to learn the craft. Conservation is more art than science, and the art is learned through practice over time and appreciation for how others do it.

By practice I mean time in the trenches, with all the hard knocks and lessons that come from the

Foreword

myriad failures and all-too-rare triumphs. The practice is learning from mentors. Brock was one of mine, and in these pages I gained a deeper background of where and how Brock learned his craft.

When I say appreciation, I mean careful understanding and respect for the work of others around you. As an artist has a special appreciation for the painting they see on the wall, in this work you learn to respect those who are good at the craft. While we've often been on opposite sides, Sandra is good at the craft, the art of this work. I've seen her at work up close and, again, in these pages I've gained a deeper background to her personal journey, as well as being reminded that there are many ways to love a place.

There are many who know Hells Canyon better than me. Idaho has many spectacular gems, and for me, Hells Canyon is one of my least explored. I'm planning to get to know it better.

Hells Canyon is a very special place for Chris Carlson. Like many, I met Chris through Cecil Andrus, Years ago I watched Andrus introduce Chris as a son. They are that close and were up to the day of Andrus' passing on August 24, 2017. Knowing Andrus as I did, that's no small honor and speaks of personal attributes and values developed over a career where the boss served as Governor of Idaho and Secretary of the Interior. Andrus will always be one of the West's extraordinary leaders and Chris was a part of that legendary team.

You're likely holding this book because Hells Canyon is your special place. However Hells Canyon speaks to you, there is much more than the majesty of the balsamroot-covered canyon walls rising up to the massive snowy peaks of the Seven Devils. There's more to fill those nights than the rumbling river and carpet of stars.

There is a story. There is a story of how Hells Canyon was saved, a story about this special place and special people who care about it.

    Brock Evans has written that "real epics, are not about the deeds of gods and goddesses...Epics are what ordinary people do, rising to scary and demanding occasions and stumbling through them no matter what."

    Hells Canyon has epic written all over it. One of the West's great rivers slices through it. The rising bluffs and mountains create one of the deepest gorges in North America. The Seven Devils look down from a height of 7,000 feet above the Snake. But the real epic is in the story of the people who love the place, and of those who worked to save it.

Rick Johnson has been the executive director of the Idaho Conservation League since 1995. His work on behalf of wild places like the Boulder-White Clouds and the Owyhee Canyonlands has carried him from trails and rivers of Idaho to the Oval Office of the White House.

INTRODUCTION

A MASS IN HELL took place in Hells Canyon on April 6, 2008. The officiating priest was Father Steve Dublinski, then vicar general for administration in the Spokane diocese, rector of the Cathedral of Our Lady of Lourdes in downtown Spokane, my pastor, friend and one hell of a fine fly fisherman. In July of 2017, he became pastor of Pullman's Sacred Heart Catholic Parish.

I had introduced him to the sacred rites of this most exclusive fraternity of fly fisherman a few years earlier, but Father Steve quickly passed me in knowledge and skill. In no way could I claim to be his teacher, nor did I. Largely self-taught, Father Steve approached the challenge with the kind of diligence one might associate with a medieval monk who had stumbled across a major remnant of one of the lost Gnostic gospels.

Before six months had elapsed he was tying his own flies. Nonetheless, I felt rewarded for being the midwife to this new holy alliance Father Steve had embraced so easily, leading to many wonderful Wednesdays during which he and I would stalk the wily westslope cutthroat up and down the reaches of the nearby St. Joe River or the North Fork of the Coeur d'Alene.

Wednesday was Father Steve's day off and it quickly became the day of the week *verboten* for anyone to schedule anything on my calendar. I also introduced Father Steve to some of the fine literature surrounding his new found hobby. Of course his favorite was A *River Runs Through It* by the Montana born and raised professor of English at the University of Chicago, Norman Maclean.

Father Steve is a Chicago native himself, having

been born there on June 26, 1955. While still very young, his family moved to Walla Walla where Father Steve attended mass at St. Patrick's Parish and received his early education at the Catholic high school, DeSales. Though more noted for its phenomenally successful football and baseball programs (at one point DeSales had captured ten small school baseball championships), Father Steve, tall (six foot five) and lean, was a key starter on the basketball team.

Even in high school, though, it was clear to fellow students that this Dublinski (Steve has six other siblings) was a cut above in terms of keen intellect and his interest in philosophy and religion. From DeSales, he attended and received his B.A. from Spokane's Gonzaga University.

While attending Gonzaga, he decided to enter the priesthood, a path which required six more years of education, four of which he spent studying in Rome. While there, Father Steve discovered, and to this day loves, Italian food and enjoys preparing it for dinner guests.

A mass on a beautiful Sunday morning in early April, as well as a delicious dinner featuring pasta carbonara are but two of the many great stories emanating from Hells Canyon, whether one hikes it, floats it, goes hunting, fishing, or engages in a Sunday sightseeing excursion in a jet boat.

That Hells Canyon is a special place cannot be denied. That many stories are generated by visitors knowingly or unknowingly captured by its magic, likewise cannot be denied. The canyon's over-arching story, though, has seldom been told in its entirety.

This book's goal is to tell the story of Hells Canyon and how it achieved protection. The story unfolds largely through my eyes and the eyes of two key players – Brock Evans from the Sierra Club and Sandra Mitchell from the Hells Canyon Alliance.

Introduction

I have a theory that most people would much rather read about other people and how they changed their world, rather than read a dry text on how an issue came about. The ideal, of course, is to find people whose life narratives help tell a story and to provide insight into how they helped to shape that story. The Hells Canyon story could perhaps find better story tellers,

Father Steve Dublinski who held a "mass in hell." Photo: Marcia Carlson

but that remains to be seen. The other purpose of this narrative is to explain the politics involved in bringing resolution to this matter. The story is one that takes time to develop and mature.

Use of a religious motif is tempting. In the beginning I thought about naming the book "Mass in Hell." It would have been a catchy title that would inspire a prospective buyer to pause while perusing a bookshelf. Once the religious motif is invoked, however, it became all too easy to carry it through the text in other ways. Thus, the initial notion was dropped.

The story told herein will focus on the politics of Hells Canyon and the politicians. Did the political figures shape the issue, or did the issue shape or define politicians, for better or worse? A reader can draw his or her own conclusion after reading through a story that is admittedly heavy on politics.

For more than twenty years, the annual hiking season for the Carlson clan started with a trek into or through Hells Canyon of the Snake River. It's the deepest gash in North America's crust, almost 7,000 feet from the rim of the canyon near Dry Diggins Lookout. The river below forms part of the boundary between the coastal states of Washington and Oregon and the mountain state of Idaho for over 100 miles.

In part, we enjoyed hiking or backpacking in Hells Canyon because spring always seemed to have arrived there two weeks earlier than anyplace else in the northwest. This particular year (2008) we had invited Father Steve to accompany us – us being several members of the Carlson family along with several members of our former Bainbridge Island neighbors, the Rick Richards family.

All were delighted when Father Steve let us know he could come. Some years we would arrive at the trailhead at Upper Pittsburg Landing and backpack the six miles upriver to the old sheep ranch owned by former Idaho Governor and U.S. Senator Len B. Jordan, and his wife, Grace.

The ranch house, bunk house and several old outbuildings stood beside Kirkwood Creek near the upriver end of Kirkwood Bar. Since 1976 the canyon, as well as several historic ranches, has been protected through its designation as a National Recreation Area. The river itself is protected by all three designations contained within the Wild and Scenic Rivers Act.

At the Jordan Ranch, a large horse pasture provides ample camping space and there are five picnic tables and five fire grates which one wants to get there early enough to claim. The prize is the grate closest to the creek, which, swollen by spring snow melt, is usually roaring down the draw, past the ranch buildings and into the Snake adjacent to where the jet boats, commercial and private, land to unload hikers, tourists on day trips up from Lewiston, and campers like our party.

That particular year we had opted to book passage

Introduction

with *Beamer's Landing*, a charter service operating out of Lewiston and Clarkston, to bring our party up to the Jordan Ranch rather than hiking in. We could have chartered a jet boat service based at the Hells Canyon Dam, which for a modest fee will come down the river and pick parties up and ferry them thirty-three miles back up stream to Granite Creek, four miles from the dam. There one can begin the best hike of all – traversing the most scenic areas in the canyon as one hikes back downriver to the Jordan Ranch and onto the trail head at Upper Pittsburg Landing.

We'd done this several times, but not this time, largely out of deference to the Stage IV neuroendocrine cancer I had been diagnosed with in November 2005. Still engaged in my personal battle to manage the cancer for many years, come hell or high water, I was in no shape to hike in, but once in the canyon at the ranch I could take short hikes and fish for bass.

That particular weekend the weather in Hells Canyon was typically April: blustery and ever-changing. There had been few sunbreaks during the day and a cool wind was blowing down river as we lit the fire in the grate on the campsite we had established in the old horse pasture. It was a minor miracle that Father Steve was able to make an extraordinary and tasty pasta carbonara with the temperature dropping into the low 40's and a light rain falling.

On Sunday morning we arose to the sounds of chukars clucking in the hills, blue sky, warm sunshine and no breeze. It felt like another Easter morning with the promise of spring and summer overwhelming the senses. At 8:30 a.m., Father Steve laid out a vestment made in Italy and a chalice made in Mexico. A large rock in the corner of the pasture served as the altar in this cathedral of the great outdoors and seven people took part in the most sacred ritual of all – the celebration of the life, death and resurrection of our lord and savior, Jesus Christ. During the prayers of the faithful, I thanked God for the wonderful blessings my family and I enjoy, but added a special thanks for that day and all those there.

It seemed to me that only in Idaho could such a special event like a Mass in Hell occur.

Hells Canyon itself is an extraordinary place with a fascinating history dating back to prehistoric times when members of aboriginal tribes and family clans sought refuge from winter storms deep within the several side canyons. They constructed earth homes a mile or so up creek ravines that flow through narrow canyons into the river.

Almost always the earth houses (a combination of digging several feet down into the earth before constructing the overhead superstructure) faced south to absorb warmth and energy from the sun. By locating a ways up these ravine canyons, they were often able to avoid the bone-chilling winds that ran up and down the river as well as across the canyon rim during the colder months of the year.

To this day there are several Indian petroglyph sites that can easily be spotted from the river trail. Cort Conley's book, *Snake River in Hells Canyon* (Backeddy Books, 1979), which does an excellent job of documenting what can be seen and visited by hiking the length of the entire river trail, provides easy directions for those who wish to see these sites.

This book, however, tells stories about the people who had a hand in bringing the Hells Canyon into the nation's system of national recreation areas so that the various assets could be protected for posterity.

My former boss, the late Governor Cecil D. Andrus, had a favorite saying about success having a thousand fathers and mothers and failure being a bastard. This book will give due credit to many of these heroes, but it

Introduction

Indian petroglyphs just off of Snake River Trail. Photo: Steve Lee

will also focus more closely on people who can be called the true saviors of Hells Canyon. Use of the religious imagery is deliberate. For many, experiencing Hells Canyon is similar to a transformative religious conversion. First among all the "saviors" is Brock Evans of the Sierra Club and much of this book tells how he brought about this miracle.

    Other stories will receive their due. In telling the story of the conflict between private power and public power interests that threatened the canyon, one must delve into the role played by Idaho's first woman representative in Congress, Gracie Pfost, who represented Idaho's First District for ten years from 1952 to 1962.

    To deal with Congresswoman Pfost and her support for public power's interest in building a single high dam in Hells Canyon is to reckon with a force of nature. She intimidated the young Frank Church when he

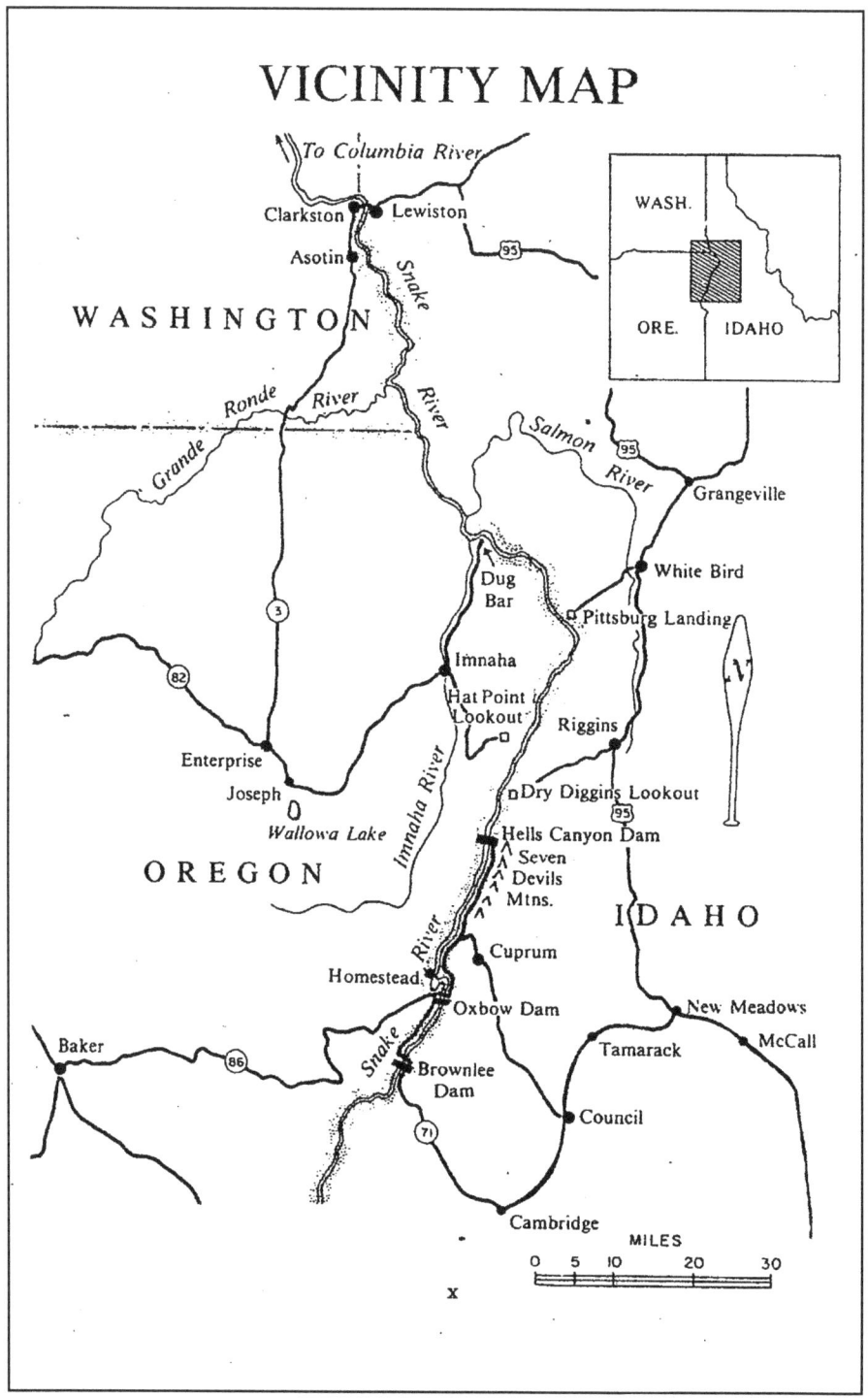

Introduction

arrived to take his Senate seat in 1957. Former Governor and U.S. Senator Len B. Jordan and his pro-private power dam proposal has to be probed in more depth when one realizes he and spouse, Grace, lived in Hells Canyon with their three children for eight years during the Depression.

To stand at the ranch today and realize the surface of the proposed High Mountain Sheep's reservoir would have been some 200 feet above has to cause one to wonder just how Len Jordan could have rationalized accepting that.

From the surprisingly voluminous material that exists on and about Hells Canyon I have selected three primary sub-stories, which I will recount from my vantage point with my perspective as well as bias. There is the public power vs. private power conflict; the National Recreation Area designation vs. the National Park designation. And then there's the conflict between the rafters and the jet boaters.

As always the focus throughout will be on the people who created policies and ultimately protection. After all, it is the individuals involved who make the policy; policies do not make people. Besides, people are far more interesting, so my goal is to tell a story through a description of its participants.

We begin with an overview of the issue, the context and circumstances, and the Carlson clan's introduction to the Snake River and Hells Canyon – and how it was love at first sight.

OVERVIEW

FOR OVER 20 YEARS, our family's first spring outing into the wonderful wilds of Idaho has been a trip into the Hells Canyon National Recreation Area. Even in 2006 and 2007, at the height of my battle against a stage IV cancer, I jet boated to the Jordan Ranch and camped overnight in the old horse pasture beside Kirkwood Creek.

We always tried to get there early enough in the day that we could claim the campsite on top of the bench, closest to the creek, because it had a picnic table where we could set our food and packs, and by lantern-light, play cards at night with a fire roaring in the nearby grate. Additionally, the site's over-hanging limbs from tall hackberry bushes were perfect for supporting a light tarp that served to keep us dry in the event of rain.

Most importantly, it was the campsite closest to the biffy and that was no small for the women in our contingent. Visiting the site over the years, we watched the Forest Service install several iterations of toilet: from the basic, old backwoods outhouse to a solar-driven waste recycler to a modern two-bathroom model one might find at any Idaho rest area.

In the last couple of years – with each visit I thought it would be the last time – I would see the rays of the evening sun crawl up "Old Shark Tooth," the large overhanging hillock that looms above the former sheep ranch to its south. Each year since the April 6, 2008, I have given thanks for another opportunity to revel in the stark beauty of the place, hearing the chukars, watching for elk on the ridges high above the river and catching bass while listening to the quiet flow and occasional

Looking from Snake River Trail down on horse pasture at the Jordan Ranch, Kirkwood Bar. Photo: Marcia Carlson

gurgling of the Snake steadily flowing north towards its mergers with the Salmon and the Clearwater rivers.

When younger and in better health, I sometimes made ten backpacking trips a season. Almost always the season began at Upper Pittsburg Landing and from there we would hike the six miles along the river trail to the Jordan Ranch at Kirkwood Bar and set up a base camp. After signing the register in the old museum that had once been a bunkhouse, I would take day hikes north or south along the river or up the draw a mile to the Carter Mansion, once the home of the canyon's best bootlegger.

Other times we would charter a jet boat to come down from the Hells Canyon Dam and pick us up at Upper Pittsburg Landing. It would take us 33 miles upstream where we would get off just below Granite Creek, four miles downstream from the dam. It would take three or four days to hike back down to the trailhead, camping along the way with the last stop for the night always being the Jordan Ranch.

Overview

Since it was usually early in the hiking season, it was often cool in the canyon. Some days, however, would be quite warm, and feel almost like a visit to the greater Phoenix area for spring training baseball in March. At that time of the season, we didn't have to worry about rattlesnakes, but we did have to keep our eyes out for poison ivy, hard to recognize when there are no leaves yet on the plant. To this point, unfortunately, I can bear painful witness.

The family's first introduction to the wonders of Hells Canyon, however, was a four-day August float trip in 1988 through the canyon with the Mike Patterson family. *Northwest Voyageurs* (then based in Lucile) served as our outfitter and guide. We put into the river below the Hells Canyon Dam and pulled out at Pittsburg Landing four days later following a leisurely fun-filled trip.

I vowed to return often and have kept that promise. I had become acquainted with Patterson when we both resided on Bainbridge Island. We shared a Catholic faith and together, with Patterson as president and me as vice president of the St. Cecilia's Parish Council, we led a successful drive to build a new church.

Patterson is one of the most talented attorneys I have ever met. He loves trial work and to my knowledge has never lost a case and he has had some of the toughest one could imagine. He also has "the Midas touch," which means every investment he makes turns to gold. This talent coupled with hard work and plenty of smarts has made him one of the wealthiest "super lawyers" in the Northwest.

When he called to suggest our two families combine to buy out all of the seats on the rafts it was a no-brainer. Considerably enhancing the trip was the availability in 1988 of Cort Conley's fine book, *The Snake River in Hells Canyon*, which painstakingly documents what there is to see every mile through the Wild and

Scenic River portion of the Canyon. The book also identifies other sites from the Jordan Ranch on Kirkwood Bar to Heller Bar where the Grande Ronde River flows into the Snake. Conley's account of these early years and some of the colorful characters who inhabited the canyon is alone worth purchasing the book.

That first raft trip was memorable for how low, slow and warm the river was. A few rapids were still rough and enjoyable and required care and caution. Others were manageable enough to permit us to body surf through them.

At times, like the lazy days of August, when the flows are low, and the current weak, and the water warm, the Snake River as it passes through the canyon appears deceptively benign. However, there always remain a few rapids where the stream bed has narrowed, increasing the pressure and the pull, all of this occurring above a deep hole.

As is the case anytime one is in the wilderness, a "wild and scenic" river can be unforgiving of any mistake, whether of choice or chance. There is a risk many are willing to take for the opportunity to be in and a part of the wild Idaho that is what most of America was before the first European explorers arrived. It is also why every person on a rafting excursion managed by an outfitter and guide service signs a liability waiver.

The closest a good friend of mine, the internationally renowned mountaineer John Roskelley, has ever come to meeting his maker was not some accident while climbing Mt. Everest or the numerous other Himalayan Mountains he has ascended. It was a rafting accident on Idaho's Lochsa River. His raft flipped in white water and he was pinned below a tree hidden under the water.

This is a rafter's worst nightmare and the greatest fear for any guide. The city of Coeur d'Alene and many of its residents were shaken to the core when, while on a trip down the main Salmon in July of 2013, a popular doctor, Maj Sturmo Gipson, came around a bend in the river in her rubber kayak and was swept into a fallen tree.

She and the kayak entangled in the branches with the flow sufficiently strong to keep her pinned underneath, causing her to drown as her husband and family frantically tried to reach and free her.

In John Roskelley's case, he was able to free himself and get to the surface in the nick of time. Most are not so lucky.

Years ago I failed to heed a guide's instructions while approaching some large rapids in Hells Canyon. Instead of following the rafts to the river's right, I went to the left, straight to and through the worst part. I was flipped out of the rubber kayak. I vividly recall the water pressure, despite my life jacket, forcing me down, down, down ever deeper into the hole. Finally, the buoyancy of the life-vest shot me to the surface; I gasped for a breath of air.

Immediately, another wave hit me and I took in water not air. A whirlpool caught me and pulled me down, again. I realized I was in serious trouble. Had there been a tree underneath to snag me, I would not be telling this tale today. Luckily, I popped back to the surface and swam over to one of the rafts, for a narrow escape. There was a sobering silence as I was pulled into the raft.

When I arrived in Washington, D.C., in January 1971, I met all the Idaho congressional delegation. Frank Church was the senior senator having been elected in 1957. A well-known liberal, his hero was the iconic William E. Borah whose oratory was second to none and who was Idaho's dominant political figure for much of the first half of the 20th century.

Len Jordan was the junior senator (having taken his seat in 1962), but Church always showed great deference to Jordan and the former governor, likewise, held Church in high regard despite their differing political persuasions. Such was the respect each had for the other that while they would always "endorse" their party's nominee against the other, neither would actively campaign against the other.

Tall, silver haired, sun wrinkled of brow and face, Jordan looked every inch the former rancher who ran sheep in Hells Canyon for eight years during the Depression.

Grace Jordan, the senator's talented, well-educated spouse, had written a slightly fictionalized account of their years in the canyon, entitled *Home Below Hells Canyon*, I quickly read it. The book is fun, informative and interesting. It has gone through 20 printings and ironically served as a foil to her husband's support for private power to construct High Mountain Sheep Dam.

Little did I know how much of my time in later years would be taken up with writing about and tangentially participating in efforts to suitably protect much of Hells Canyon.

In 2010, I wrote two columns about Hells Canyon. One on May 5, about the annual pilgrimage into the canyon, and the other on May 12, about then Interior Secretary Walter J. Hickel's 1969 float trip through Hells Canyon. Hickel's trip was a sophisticated lobbying effort put together by two of the Northwest's early conservation leaders, Boyd Norton, from *Friends of the Earth*, and Brock Evans of *the Sierra Club*.

Working with Governor Andrus' future natural resource aide, John Hough (then the news anchor and one man news bureau for Lewiston's KLEW-TV), the group enticed CBS television personality Arthur Godfrey and folksinger Burl Ives to be the celebrity "hooks" that succeeded in landing the interior secretary's participation. It was a true publicity coup and helped

Overview

Old "Shark Tooth" Rock that looms over Jordan ranch house and bunkhouse, Kirkwood Bar. Photo: Marcia Carlson

other efforts to advertise the importance of protecting the area from future development. The primary audience, of course, was the United States Congress.

I called the May 12 column "Hickel's Trip Through Hell," which was done to attract attention to the historical retelling rather than characterize the trip. Hickel emerged from the August trip a solid convert for federal protection, but just what form that protection would take was not yet clear. Nonetheless, in late August, Hickel let it be known the Interior Department was changing its position and was going to oppose the High Mountain Sheep dam.

I believe there are no coincidences in politics, so it seems likely the switch may have had more to do with Brock Evans having been to the White House in July and visiting both John Erlichman, a senior aide to President Nixon, and Russell Train, then the undersecretary at Interior. Evans left the meetings confident he had won a couple of converts.

Because Hells Canyon is difficult to reach by car, some people may wonder today why the canyon needed protection. The answer, in part, is something Andrus identified early in his consideration of protected status for Hells Canyon, and also the Sawtooth Mountains of central Idaho. Many in the conservation movement immediately thought that the Sawtooths and Hells Canyon needed the highest degree of protection possible and so sought to add them to the nation's National Park System.

Governor Andrus and Senator Jim McClure both thought otherwise. They told all who asked that a "national park" designation would result in the areas being "loved to death." Early in his first term as governor, Andrus favored a lesser, but sufficient form of protection called a "National Recreation Area." Such a designation would allow continued compatible uses and would not lock up the area like National Park status would have.

Andrus and McClure knew folks would still want to hunt in areas within a proposed NRA. Park status in the lower 48 states usually did not allow hunting. They also knew that carefully buying up grazing leases over time and phasing out sheep herding was the only way to secure the cooperation of the state's influential ranching and sheep raising industry. Both knew how important it was to get people together on the ground level and listen to each other in a give-and-take process that hopefully would lead to consensus.

Brock Evans and many in the Sierra Club, as well as the Hells Canyon Preservation Council, always expressed deep regret they did not hold out for national park status for Hells Canyon and the Idaho's Sawtooth Mountains. Evans felt it was a specious argument to say that park status would have created a Yosemite National Park situation replete with traffic jams that rivaled an LA freeway at rush hour.

Overview

Evans believed that the relative accessibility for both Hells Canyon and the Sawtooths, but especially Hells Canyon, would always serve as a deterrent to being overrun by hordes of tourists. Evans also knew that any bill passing Congress and creating a Hells Canyon national park would have had language permitting hunting either throughout the new park or in "park preserves" which was the park service euphemism for areas allowing hunting.

Evans further reminded any listener that 98% of the land area in a national park would have an overlay of a wilderness designation. He accepted that National Parks have a mystique to them that would draw visitors from all over – that people do and would love them, but not to death as conjured by Andrus and McClure.

However, most of those wanting national park status conceded that it would be folly to fight the combined support Andrus and McClure could bring to bear if they so desired. Thus, the tactical decision to accept less than a full loaf was accepted.

In Hells Canyon, Andrus and McClure also knew there would be conflict with those who favored floating through the canyon as opposed to those who favored utilization by jet boat. Both interests had to be accommodated, even on whatever portion of the Snake River below Hells Canyon Dam received the highest degree of protection under the federal Wild and Scenic River Act.

The biggest threat to Hells Canyon preservation was the effort by private hydro-power interests to build one more "high" dam in the canyon near the confluence of the Snake and Salmon rivers.

This dam, to be called High Mountain Sheep, would have created a reservoir extending upstream to the base of the Hells Canyon Dam and would have flooded some of the most spectacular places along the river, including the

Jordan Ranch at Kirkwood Bar.

As noted in the *Introduction*, one of the biggest advocates of the dam, incredibly, was Idaho's junior senator and former governor, Len Jordan. I have never understood how Jordan, who I greatly admire, could support flooding over the old homestead. Perhaps it was a form of "familiarity can breed contempt" – that is when one lives in a place for many years one can discount its unique qualities and cease to recognize how special it may be.

As with all subjects controversial, luck plays a role. In this case, the continuing controversy swirling through the Pacific Northwest in the 1950s and 1960s, the conflict between public and private power, caused a fortunate delay in commencing construction of the proposed dam.

Public power, as represented by the Bonneville Power Administration, which markets the power output of federal dams along the Columbia and Lower Snake rivers, finally had been checked by Idaho Power and its allies. They succeeded in getting a federal license to build the Oxbow, Brownlee, and Hells Canyon dams on the upper part of what was called the Middle Snake River Reach.

In order to delay the proposed High Mountain Sheep dam, Senator Frank Church convinced Jordan that there should be a moratorium on the granting of any permit, or of legislation from the Congress, until various on-going studies by several federal agencies had been completed. Church thought a ten year moratorium was called for. Jordan supported him and much to the surprise of Evans and his colleagues, the Idaho Senators announced their intentions.

Not only would this allow the studies to be completed, and done more thoroughly, it also bought time for the environmental community to continue to muster support for a Hells Canyon National Park designation that would provide "wild and scenic" status for twenty miles of the river through the canyon. Most importantly, it prohibited any further dam building.

Both Idaho senators supported a seven-year moratorium (three years had gone by since they first proposed a ten year moratorium ending in 1978) on dam building while the studies were completed, hearings held, and the public educated about the stakes and options.

Personalities almost always play a part in these legislative dances and it became clear that Oregon Senator Bob Packwood rubbed not only Idaho's senators the wrong way, but also Oregon's senior senator, Mark Hatfield. Packwood had introduced a preservation bill in the spring of 1971, primarily written by Brock Evans, that would serve as a substitute for the Church and Jordan moratorium. The two Idaho senators and Hatfield quickly made it clear that Packwood's bill was going nowhere fast.

As a "compromise" and a courtesy, the Senate Interior Committee chairman, Washington Senator Henry M. Jackson, had the subcommittee chair, Nevada Senator Allan Bible, announce that he would hold a hearing on Packwood's bill in the fall. Packwood then withdrew his substitute bill and the Senate passed the Church/Jordan moratorium almost unanimously.

That September I was one of the few reporters attending the hearing, having been retained by the *Lewiston Tribune* to provide spot coverage. Green as I was, I saw that in response to Packwood's refusal to include language guaranteeing primacy of upstream water rights had effectively killed the bill.

The net effect isolated Packwood, ensuring he would be nothing but a bit player in the passage of any bill. The combined clout of Jackson, Jordan, Hatfield and Church was too much for Packwood and his influence soon faded.

In the meantime, Idaho's First District

congressman, Jim McClure (the front-runner to succeed Len Jordan who had announced his retirement plans in August 1971) continued to vacillate on whether to support any moratorium on the Middle Snake. Strongly supported by Idaho Power and other hydroelectric interests, McClure was sympathetic to the business side of the equation and somewhat unfriendly to those espousing the Senate moratorium.

What turned the future senator around was his own mail-in survey. While not truly scientific, McClure put great stock in these self-identifying surveys. Much to his surprise, a solid majority of the respondents indicated support for a dam building moratorium and creation of a "wild and scenic" river designation. In September, the first district congressman started singing a different tune.

About this time, Idaho's senior senator was attacked by the environmental community for his support of the moratorium on the Middle Snake. Boyd Norton, a former Idahoan then living in Colorado, sharply criticized Church in *Not Man Apart*, the newspaper of *Friends of the Earth*. Calling the moratorium a "sell out," Norton also criticized Church for "almost vindictively" opposing Senator Packwood's Hells Canyon NRA bill.

Church turned the other cheek, refusing to respond to the personal attack on his integrity, and brushed it off by saying he still felt they were working toward the same objective. As 1971 wound to a close some observers thought the state's environmental community looked like they were losing badly on three issues:

1. Legislation creating a Hells Canyon NRA was going nowhere because of Packwood's less than adroit handling of it and Senator Church pushing the moratorium issue.
2. Legislation creating a Sawtooth NRA was sidetracked, let alone a Sawtooth National Park

bill, because of questions surrounding whether the White Clouds and Boulder Mountains should be given wilderness protection.
3. Despite a delay in the opening of bids, the Interior Department's Bureau of Reclamation was proceeding with its plans for the Teton Dam to be built on a prime fly fishing stream in southeastern Idaho. The project was strongly supported in Idaho and by the entire congressional delegation, as well as by Governor Andrus.

Evans disagreed strongly with those who thought the environmental community was behind the eight ball and in a losing position. Rather, he believed his efforts, and those of the Hells Canyon Preservation Council, had succeeded in elevating the need to protect Hells Canyon to the national level. What had begun was an ongoing national debate which was attracting national media attention. Evans did not share Boyd Norton's angry views regarding Senator Church and the moratorium bill. Instead he viewed the move by Church as an adroit action to avoid taking sides until there was a clearer expression of support or non-support by Idahoans.

Evans later said he felt the moratorium hurt the cause, especially the cause of those seeking national park status, because it slowed down their momentum. "To us a moratorium just kicked the can down the road, took away our momentum, undercut our national publicity and who knew what would happen when the moratorium expired?"

As 1972 opened, Church let it be known that his first priority would be getting the Sawtooth NRA established by legislation with additional wilderness acreage added and, including resolution of the status of the White Clouds and the Boulders. The senator wanted a Sawtooth-White Clouds NRA. In addition, Church said there would be language withdrawing the proposed NRA from any further mineral entries under the 1872 Mining Law.

In late January of 1972, the House passed a Sawtooth Wilderness bill, 369 to 9. Despite the lopsided margin, Church immediately said it would have to be modified significantly. In particular, Church believed the Sawtooth Peaks had to be in the NRA, not part of a separate wilderness area. A wilderness designation for the White Clouds and Boulder Mountains at that time would have allowed possible additional mineral entries until 1983 under amendments that took precedence as part of the 1964 Wilderness Act.

Of course it was not lost on some observers that the 1964 Wilderness Act had been carried by the same Frank Church.

One of the nine members of Congress voting no was Republican John Saylor of Pennsylvania. Saylor was a member of the Sierra Club who believed the Sawtooths warranted national park status. He also claimed his view was shared by major environmental groups in Idaho and by Governor Andrus. Saylor was correct in his belief that the Sawtooths merited national park status, but was wrong regarding Andrus' purported support.

Andrus had consistently supported an NRA designation over a national park designation, much to the chagrin of his friend, Paul Fritz, the supervisor of Idaho's Craters of the Moon National Monument. In September of 1967, following a hike through the Boulder Mountains and the White Clouds, Evans proposed that a 900,000+ acre national park be created. He contended that the area truly merited the national park designation.

No member of the Idaho delegation, however, agreed, nor did Governor Andrus, who consistently believed that national park status would have resulted in the area being "loved to death."

Much of the political maneuvering throughout 1972

was driven by the forthcoming election of a new senator from Idaho. Conventional wisdom favored Congressman McClure in the GOP primary, and his political director, Jim Goller, a savvy and crafty political practitioner, was not about to give a more conservative primary opponent, former Second District Congressman George Hansen, an opening to come after McClure.

McClure skillfully played to those who wanted a dam-building moratorium on the Snake by crafting a compromise with the Second District Congressman, Orval Hansen (no relation to George), the compromise went nowhere in the Senate, but gave McClure cover. In the meantime, his staff began preparing to work with Senator Church and Governor Andrus on crafting an acceptable Hells Canyon bill if McClure won the race to succeed Len Jordan.

On August 8, the state's Democrats chose popular Idaho State University President William E. "Bud" Davis as their nominee. Davis bested the three Ada County Democrats in the race, Attorney General Tony Park, Boise attorney (and later Andrus-appointed Supreme Court Judge) Byron Johnson, and Boise feminist Rose Bowman.

On the Republican side, McClure brushed aside his three challengers, former Congressman George Hansen, former Governor Robert Smylie and Glen Wegner, an Ivy League educated holder of degrees in law and medicine.

Despite the heavy Republican leaning manifesting in Idaho, Davis mounted a surprisingly strong challenge to McClure in the general election, even though McClure's campaign outspent Davis' by a 4 to 1 margin.

As 1973 began, all three major environmental issues remained in play on the Idaho political scene. My wife, Marcia, our young daughter, Alisa, and I had just moved back to our native Idaho; I had accepted an offer to become press secretary to Governor Andrus. Two years in D.C. had been enough. We had seen most of the historic sights to be seen, visited all the museums and had taken in as much history as one could absorb. It was time to come home.

Meanwhile, in a fine example of bi-partisanship and compromise, newly elected Senator Jim McClure worked constructively with Andrus, Church, and their staffs to hammer out a bill acceptable to most parties, including Oregon's Bob Packwood.

Despite his early career support for the Liberty Amendment, McClure turned out not to be the anti-wilderness, anti-protection zealot Evans and others feared he might be. Evans tells a story of having approached McClure in 1972 when he was still a congressman at a meeting in the Ketchum/Sun Valley area.

"Jim, you say you want the boundaries of the Sawtooth wilderness to be as they are now. Were you aware the Forest Service has a different idea? All their new proposed maps of the Sawtooths leave out the boundaries of two key valleys: Queens and Little Queens," Evans said to McClure.

Evans told McClure unequivocally that these areas had been deliberately removed by the Forest Service and Evans said he had hiked the area the year before which clarified the Forest Service's reasoning. "They are chock full of giant old ponderosa pines and the Forest Service wants to log them," Evans stated.

McClure promised to look into it, did so and found out that Evans was correct. McClure then saw that they were included within the wilderness boundaries. Evans was forever grateful to Jim McClure.

One of my favorite memories from Andrus' first go-round as governor was watching he and McClure on their hands and knees in the Governor's Office poring over a big map of the Hells Canyon area. They were drawing boundaries that represented hydrological divides, areas where domestic sheep could roam and areas where they could not and identifying stretches of the Snake River below Hells Canyon Dam to be protected under different designations.

Both men had hiked, fished, and/or hunted in the area. They knew what they were talking about and could visualize the topography. By no stretch of the imagination were they drawing arbitrary lines on a map. It remains indelibly imprinted in my mind as a fine example of two of Idaho's leading political figures working in tandem for the public good, while preserving historic and scenic recreation values.

Compromise carried the day with the Sawtooth NRA with the exception that a wilderness designation for the Boulders and White Clouds had to be postponed to a later date. The Sawtooth National Forest administration was charged with continuing to manage under the multiple-use doctrine, but in a manner that would preserve the area's scenic and historic values.

None of the major players are still alive. Senator Church died in 1984, Senator McClure died in 2012. Governor Andrus passed away in August 2017.

Surprisingly, picking up the mantle of congressional leadership on this issue has been the Republican congressman from Idaho's Second District, former Idaho House Speaker and Blackfoot dentist Mike Simpson. In an unholy alliance, Simpson has worked closely with Idaho Conservation League Executive Director Rick Johnson to secure passage of a new wilderness bill affording protection for the high mountain peak areas of the Boulders and the White Clouds.

A little noted side issue that emerged during the 1970s debate on the fate of the Sawtooths, the White Clouds, and Hells Canyon was the relentless march to the construction of the Teton Dam. Most environmentalists in Idaho opposed the project, but with the exception of activists around Idaho Falls, like Pete Henault and Russ Brown, few made it their priority.

Shortly after the dam was completed and the reservoir behind filled, the dam collapsed on June 5, 1976, with a loss of eleven lives and damage to property and crops totaling hundreds of millions of dollars.

The day it failed Governor Andrus had set aside time to fly into the Idaho backcountry with his good friend, Rex Lanham, who owned and operated a fly-in lodge on Cabin Creek. Andrus planned on getting some restful fly fishing accomplished while restoring his batteries for a few days. Needless to say, he canceled the trip upon hearing the news of the dam failure and immediately flew over to the site of the collapse.

Thirty-six years later, some farmers in the impacted area wanted to reauthorize and construct a better built dam. Incredibly, they seemed to have forgotten what happened the first time.

There are enough people with long enough memories who oppose reauthorization. A 2011 poll indicated there was sufficient opposition so that members of the congressional delegation, as well as Governor Butch Otter, elected in 2006, felt the risk did not supersede any possible reward.

Such is the influence of the "Committee of Nine" water masters of the Upper Snake projects that Otter nonetheless felt feasibility of a new project should be studied and, unlike Andrus, would not rule out a new dam.

It appears as if Otter may not understand the reach and pull of today's environmental community. Even in Idaho, it can quickly develop and distribute messages, generate massive e-mail and phone call campaigns to congressional offices, in order to influence an issue.

The most important, but little noted, consequence of the dam's failure was the tendency of Andrus to more sharply scrutinize cost-benefit claims made by proponents of such projects. While he always believed some dams fulfill a legitimate and immediate need for hydro-power or high head irrigation, he knew many projects had numbers that were "mickey-moused" to create better justifications.

Because of the Teton Dam experience, Andrus was able to exercise a more critical and credible review of the proposed projects and of those projects that had been built. In particular, he started increasing his criticism of the four lower Snake River dams, the last of which was completed in 1973. In speaking at the final dam dedication, *The Lewiston Tribune* reported his public questioning as to whether the Corps (U.S. Army Corps of Engineers) really understood the adverse impact the Lower Snake dams would have on downstream salmon and steelhead smolt migration.

Few folks recalled that earlier in 1973 Andrus, with a look of pure joy captured by *Lewiston Tribune* photographer Barry Kough, had dynamited a small regulating dam near Lewiston owned by what was then called Washington Water Power Co. Its removal restored the Clearwater to the exclusive list of those rare U.S. Rivers without a single dam.

In later years, Andrus also bemoaned in his political biography, *Politics Western Style*, and in "historical look-backs," his support of the four lower Snake River dams and the Dworshak Dam on the North Fork of the Clearwater. He recognized well after the fact how much excellent elk habitat and how many quality cutthroat streams had been sacrificed on the altar of the Bonneville Power Administration and the Army Corps of Engineers.

Andrus also recognized that had he opposed Dworshak Dam and the four Lower Snake dams, he might not have been elected as the State Senator from Clearwater County for much of the 60s. Given his lasting impact on issues he championed while in public office, I, for one, would accept the trade-off as a net-gain for the environment.

As the evidence mounted of the devastating impacts of the four Lower Snake projects on Idaho's prized and valuable salmon and steelhead runs, it became clear to Andrus that a "bad trade off" had been made. Upon his return to the governorship in 1987, he started formulating the elements of a fish flush plan on the Snake that would emulate nature's spring flow critical to quickly carrying the salmon and steelhead smolt to the sea.

This, too, became controversial but Andrus was a formidable debater on these matters and emerged as the natural leader on the subject of dams and fish. As we shall see in following chapters the debate on the future of Hells Canyon, which was initially a fight between public power and private power over who would build either one high dam or three smaller dams, all too quickly evolved into a debate over whether there would be any dam.

What follows are my thoughts as I took my grandchildren up river in 2012 – their first trip and my final trip:

The large jet boat from Beamer's Hells Canyon Excursions powered its way up the Snake River against the largest cubic feet per second flow ever measured in one day on the Snake-127,000 CFS. The river, swollen by the spring runoff and an incredible amount of spring rains, was awash with more debris than long-time river watchers had ever seen. The date was April 28, 2012, I wanted to introduce our grandchildren to the canyon while I was still physically able. I wanted him and his sister, Marin, to visit the old Jordan Ranch bunkhouse, now a museum.

I wanted them to see the pictures of the Jordans and hear the story about how the long-time occupant of the ranch, who as a United States senator, tried to entice "Gramps" to be his press secretary many years back.

Overview

Mountain Sheep near Granite Creek on trail to Hibbs Ranch. Photo: Steve Lee

More than anything, I wanted them to share my sense of the wild and scenic values I had helped in a small way to preserve, to listen to the wind coming down the river, to see the wildlife along the river – the deer, the mountain sheep, the river otters – as we worked our way upstream.

They listened to the boat driver tell the story of petroglyphs etched in the rocks at Buffalo Eddy, more than 6,000 years old, and to the story of the sinking of the old Imnaha sternwheeler bringing supplies to the now gone mining village of Eureka. I wanted them to hear and react with dismay at the murder of 37 Chinese miners by outlaws looking for gold near Deep Creek in 1887.

I wanted them to visualize Chief Joseph and his fleeing band of Nez Perce warriors, women, children, dogs, cattle, and horses, fording the Snake River at Dug Bar to stay ahead of the pursuing cavalry led by the one-armed former Union general, Oliver Howard. That no lives were lost in that fording still seems a miracle.

On this particular day there was a fly-in at the narrow dirt strip on Dug Bar. A dozen Cessna 182s, smaller Pipers, and other planes lined up along the dirt strip. I made a point of explaining that one of the features of the Wilderness Act of 1964, and embedded in the act creating the Hells Canyon National Recreation Area, was language permitting continued access by airplanes and motorized crafts like jet boats, into these wilderness areas.

I explained this was done so children like them and health challenged adults like "Gramps" could still visit and enjoy these areas. I told them there were people in this world who felt access should only go to those who were hale and hearty enough to hike or backpack into the wilderness; that they should not be subjected even to the sound of aircraft flying into the various backcountry landing strips.

I told them about another United States senator from Idaho, Frank Church, who authored the Wilderness Act of 1964 and for whom one of Idaho's great wilderness areas is now named. I pointed out that he specifically had people like grandpa in mind when he wrote language guaranteeing the various backcountry air strips would be preserved also.

I mentioned how often I had flown into isolated air strips with Jim McDevitt, an extraordinary backcountry pilot who would invite Gramps to go along on fishing trips to places like Moose Creek, Shearer, the Flying B, Big Creek, and the Selway Lodge.

Despite legislative language protecting these places for entering the wilderness, I also told them about how the U.S. Forest Service, the unit of government which manages these wilderness areas, had folks hell bent on closing most of these back country air strips; that they had come up with absurd ideas like conducting Limited Acceptable Change (LAC's) studies that measured the amount of dust a plane landing might generate and then speculate that the small *amount of dust because of "cumulative" impacts might hurt the fish in the nearby streams.*

One story I did not tell them, but of which they might read or hear about someday, was that the day also marked the 39th anniversary of the drowning of a friend of mine, Eddie Williams, Andrus' first chief of staff, along with his friend, Jack Bowman. They drowned when the boat in which they were traveling swamped in the Imnaha rapids.

If I live long enough to instill in them a love for the wild and free, they will learn soon enough a need to respect the wilderness and the wilds, to be properly cautious, to be prepared to deal with the unexpected, to take responsibility for themselves and their actions, to know life can be unforgiving of some mistakes, and where one does survive a mistake to learn from it and move forward.

Soon enough they will learn there is a yin and a yang, the flip side of life, but that a life worth living is one worth taking calculated risks, that wilderness, like life itself, contains great joy and great sorrow. They will come to learn that there truly is a culture of life as well as death, a secular and selfish world along side a spiritual and a sharing one.

I hope they will be graced by The Almighty to appreciate the gifts they have, the talents they have been blessed with, the love they are surrounded by. Once in a while, I also want them to give a thought of thanks to all those preceding them who had enough foresight to preserve and protect special places where one can experience the presence of The Almighty and observe the face of God.

THE EARLY DAYS

THE FIRST THING one has to recognize is that Hells Canyon is not a pristine and unscarred place, like the Grand Canyon or Zion National Park. It is not a pristine wilderness where there are few traces of the human hand. If anything, it's quite the opposite, a unique area totally meriting the protection the U.S. Forest Service.

The late senator Len Jordan liked to call the Snake River a "working river" and the "main artery" of southern Idaho's commerce. During its almost thousand mile journey from headwaters within the boundaries of Yellowstone National Park to its confluence with the Clearwater River at Lewiston, water is withdrawn and used to nurture the potatoes for which Idaho is so famous, as well as other valuable crops.

As the 19th century turned into the 20th, it has been estimated over 2,000 people worked and derived their livelihood on or adjacent to the river from Lewiston to Payette. One might call Hells Canyon in those days a "working canyon" and indeed much different from the bottom lands of the Grand Canyon.

If one hikes the wild and scenic portion of the river (from Hells Canyon Dam to Pittsburg Landing), one views incredibly scenic vistas, especially when pausing to rest at the top of Suicide Point and to look back up river.

As scenic as these views are, the canyon was designated as a national recreation area both because of the multiple-uses permitted, such as hunting, which is not allowed in most Lower 48 national parks, and revived grazing permits. A few such permits are still issued for the summer grazing on the ridge and knolls that surround the

Seven Devils Mountains, however, grazing was banned.

Additionally, there is another less utilized but valid meaning to the word "re-create." In many respects that word covers what the U.S. Forest Service is attempting to do: *re-create* Hells Canyon as it was before the non-natives arrived to put their heavy marks on the land. This concept is difficult for us to get our minds around. We've been conditioned by the news media over the years and skillful marketing within the federal agencies to think that lands overseen by the Forest Service and the Park Service are carefully managed wild wilderness.

Few east of the Mississippi can even grasp the idea of public lands, most of which are managed by another "alphabet soup" agency, or the Bureau of Land Management. It is counter-intuitive to these folks that the Forest Service is well along a path of restoring the wild and scenic river portion of the canyon to what it was when the Lewis and Clark expedition traveled through the area in 1806.

There is a high probability that three members of the Corps of Discovery – Sergeant John Ordway, Private Robert Frazier and Private Peter Weiser – were the first white men to enter the lower part of Hells Canyon during their return trip from the Pacific coast near Astoria in 1806.

They were camped in the Clearwater Valley near present-day Kamiah for a month as high snows on the Lolo Trail return route forced them to bide their time. The search for food led these "hunter" members of the expedition to head west and into the canyon in search of a Nez Perce fishing village thought to be there. Thus, the "Ordway Expedition" began what was believed to be a short trip beginning on May 27, 1806. It turned into a seven-day expedition over rough terrain across the Camas Prairie into and out of the Salmon and Snake River canyons.

The Early Days

They did find some Nez Perce who traded salmon with them that unfortunately spoiled before they returned to the base camp on June 2, 1806.

There is ample evidence that the forefathers of today's First Nations and Native Americans inhabited parts of Hells Canyon thousands of years ago, at least during the winter because the canyon was more hospitable and warmer than the highlands and plains. Several petroglyphs have been discovered in Hells Canyon which carbon dating has indicated are over 6,000 years old.

There may have been some individual trappers who passed through the canyon in the 1820s and 1830s looking for beaver pelts. If so, history has not recorded their names. The first real influx of the "white man" came in 1860 with the discovery of gold in Oro Fino Creek near Pierce, about 75 miles due east of Lewiston. The town quickly grew, in becoming the "jumping off" point into central Idaho.

Captain John Mullan's building the Mullan Road in the 1860s linked the Inland Northwest with the Midwest. It started at Fort Walla Walla and terminated at Fort Benton on the Missouri River in Montana. Highway 10 and later part of I-90 follows Mullan's pioneering route.

It's hard to imagine Fort Benton as a port in the 1860s and 1870s, but, like Lewiston, it was also a gateway for hundreds if not thousands of prospectors seeking gold. Today, as one walks from the largely restored Union Hotel down the waterfront to view the last of the some 130 markers that have been erected to honor Mullan. There are murals and signs depicting the port at the height of its activity. One can feel the energy unleashed, imagine the hopes and dreams as the waves of gold seekers, farmers, merchants, hustlers, prostitutes, surged through this port to disperse throughout the region.

Some even found their way into Hells Canyon. The

gold they were after was there but not in abundance. Despite the paucity of gold in the canyon, the perception that a group of Chinese had discovered a bonanza near Deep Creek led to one of the worst massacres in Northwest history.

A group of outlaws and horse thieves ambushed a work force of Chinese digging at a site near the mouth of Deep Creek in a May 1887. When it was all over, 31 Chinese had been coldly murdered by these thugs. Tragically, there was no bonanza of gold to be had, the Chinese, in effect, were gathering the crumbs from an earlier effort.

Even more tragically, after law enforcement agents tracked down and arrested several of the perpetrators, not one person was convicted.

The high water mark for mining in the canyon coincided with the advent of the 20th century. Some investors decided it was a reasonable risk to build a mill on the Eureka Bar downstream from where the Imnaha River flows into the Snake. It was not a wise investment. Indeed, the probability is high that there was no return on the investment.

However, even more folks were seeing the canyon and the various spots where ranches were established on both sides of the river in the 80-mile stretch that runs downstream (and due north) from today's Hells Canyon Dam to Heller Bar. Rapid in-filling took place with many characters, carving out a living in Hells Canyon.

Cort Conley does a superb job of telling the stories of these early pioneers in his book *Snake River in Hells Canyon*. The book, published by Backeddy Press of Cambridge in 1979, is an indispensable guide for anyone desiring the colorful history of these pioneers.

Likewise, Grace Jordan, spouse of Len Jordan, relates an equally fine set of stories about her neighbors and their progeny in her classic 1954 book, *Home Below Hells Canyon*. She admits that for the sake of a good story she occasionally exercised literary license.

Many of the historic residents of the canyon appear in her book. Martin Hibbs and his family, Pete and Bud Wilson, Billy and Fred McGaffee, Dick Carter, Don Axtell, Julia Reid, Ken Johnson, Clay David, and Till Phillips. The Circle C Ranch, the Temperance Creek Ranch, and the Saddle Creek Ranch are but a few of the homesteads in the canyon that she weaves into her story.

It is a faithful account of the Jordan family living in the canyon for eight years during the Great Depression. The Jordan's then moved to Grangeville, where their three children received more formal schooling. Len purchased an auto dealership and ran for and was elected to the Idaho House of Representatives in 1946. Defeated when he ran for re-election in 1948, he nonetheless threw his hat into the race for governor in 1950, rolled over the other "wanna-be's" and defeated the Democrat nominee, Cal Wright.

By a 1944 statute a governor could not succeed himself, which meant one four-year term. After leaving the governorship in 1954, Jordan was appointed by his good friend, President Dwight D. Eisenhower, to the International Joint Commission. The IJC had been created by the Boundary Waters Treaty of 1909 between the United States and Canada as a peaceful way to resolve border disputes.

From there Len was appointed and then elected to the U.S. Senate in 1962 upon the death of Senator Henry Dworshak. He served ten years, retiring in 1972.

Both Grace and Len Jordan knew, as did their children, that one thoughtless slip when living in the canyon, far from any doctor, could be fatal. In repeating stories to their children they were reinforcing the canyon's basic rules for survival. Thus, a hike through the canyon today is to hike through remnant grain patches, and abandoned cabins with increasing admiration for the pioneer's fortitude, persistence, and work ethic. A hike in and through Hells Canyon today is more than a stroll through government lands; it is a living history journey through a time not so long ago.

As one hikes north on the river trail or floats north on rafts, or is in a jet boat, he or she becomes familiar with those who would have been their neighbors. On the Idaho side, just four miles below the Hells Canyon Dam, at Granite Creek, one can hike a mile up the draw to the Hibbs Ranch. All that remains are the foundation of the homestead.

If ambitious, one can continue up the steep ridges behind the old ranch to the canyon rim where the Hibbs had a summer-time "cow camp" close to a continuous running spring that provided water for livestock.

Further north, one could look across the Snake to the Oregon side of the river where Saddle Creek flowed into the Snake. There are the remnants of the ranch run for many years by Pete Wilson, a modern day legend who was featured in *Life Magazine* as well as being a prominent character in an article for the *Saturday Evening Post* written by future Oregon U.S. Senator Richard Neuberger.

Opposite Saddle Creek on the Idaho side, where Squaw Creek flowed into the Snake, is Billy McGaffee's cabin. Downstream one encounters Ralph Stickney's cabin above Johnson Bar. Then a hiker would come to where Sheep Creek, the origin of which is in the Seven Devils Mountains, flows into the Snake. It also is where one of the tougher rapids exists year round regardless of the river's flow. An excellent trail follows Sheep Creek from the Windy Saddle Campground high in the Seven Devils down to the confluence with the Snake. There Fred McGaffee had his home.

About a mile and a half downstream from Sheep Creek, just past Steep Creek, the trail drops down to a little cove or eddy that has a sandy beach as well as a 40-foot high cliff to build a fire against. Its easy to spot because in mid-stream there is a large rock and toward the Oregon side of the river is a fairly deep hole from which guides on river trips can usually catch large sturgeon that look like the prehistoric fish they are.

The sturgeon is a classic bottom feeder and can grow to enormous size.

It is a favorite camp site and easy to recognize because of an ocher-hued gash in the side of the canyon looming above and behind the camp site. A short distance away is Pine Creek where Floyd Harvey, who was one of the early saviors of the Canyon, had his lodge. There were seven buildings on the site leased from the Forest Service – the main lodge and cabins for guests.

Harvey was the founder of *Hells Canyon Excursions*, and between 1960 and 1965 no one fought harder to protect and preserve Hells Canyon. In 1974, an arsonist torched his lodge and cabins. The Forest Service refused to renew his lease and Harvey was out of the canyon "bed and breakfast" business, but he still had his excursion operations.

He was one of the founding members of the Hells Canyon Preservation Council and will always be near the top of the list of those who saved Hells Canyon for posterity.

Shortly after leaving the campsite, one starts a gentle climb to the top of what some call Pine Bar and others call High Bar. Though this area is mostly covered with short grass and few trees, there are interesting off trail sites, such as the Hiltsey gravesite. As one starts up the draw, he or she also sees the Meyer Creek tunnel cut through the side hill by Albert Myers many years ago.

The rancher originally envisioned tapping into the creek with a large pipe aimed slightly downhill thus employing gravity to bring water to upper Big Bar. Lower

Big Bar has a small building used by the occasional skilled back country pilot to land on the level dirt field. These pilots were usually carrying supplies for the still operating Temperance Creek Ranch on the Oregon side of the river.

Pilots would wave to get the attention of someone at the ranch. One of the hands would go down to the river, crank the engine on the small dinghy and cross the river to pick up the supplies.

A few miles more and one can rest at the top of Suicide Point some 500 feet above the river. From there one can look back up the river with a great view of the Temperance Creek Ranch and Big Bar. If the day is not cloudy, one can spot the Dry Diggins Lookout on the edge of the Seven Devils Mountains. The view is breathtaking.

Descending from Suicide Point soon leads one past Half Moon Bar. At about 2 ½ miles, one begins traversing Kirkwood Bar, riverfront of the Jordan Ranch. The long collapsed sheep-shearing building is to one's right. The old bunkhouse has been turned into a museum which warrants time and scrutiny. The ranch house is still there along with the unique bathtub Len constructed.

A Forest Service Camp monitor is usually present. As these same monitors came back year after year, we became quite fond of them, especially Don and Dawnie James, who lived in Prineville in eastern Oregon most of the year but loved their annual two-month stay at the Jordan Ranch. Don, of course, is a retired Forest Service ranger.

The last six miles from the Jordan Ranch to Pittsburg Landing starts with a steep climb from the old horse pasture up several hundred feet before the trail levels off for a few miles along the side of the canyon. There are some incredible vistas and scenic sights up and down the canyon before crossing Kirby Creek which flows into the Snake. Here one finds the only remaining private in-holding in the National Recreation Area –

Norm Riddle's two story lodge. For years Norm has run a successful jet boat operation, *Snake River Excursions*, and the Lodge is used by guests who want more than a day.

About a mile before reaching the trailhead at Upper Pittsburg Landing is Corral Creek, which has no bridge. During a late spring runoff, it requires a little wading.

Brock Evans is one of the few fans of Hells Canyon who prefers the Oregon side of the canyon. He has some solid points. First, the Oregon side has fewer access points, necessitating one to travel 50 miles or more. Along with Pete Henault and his wife, Evans and the Henaults once rode horses on the Oregon side for three days. They rarely encountered other backpackers or horse packers. The trail undulates along the canyon rising and falling 300 to 500 feet over a mile at times.

Evans says that while the views were different but just as scenic, it was hard to beat the solitude. "It's an incredible place." It seems half way between the heights of the canyon rim and the rapids on the river floor. We rode through gentle, rolling country yet there were lots of huge yellow pines, nice meadows, tumbling creeks. It was 35 miles of great beauty and it clearly qualified for wilderness status. There were no human habitations except for the Circle C Ranch – it was simply too inaccessible."

THE COMMITTEE OF NINE, IDAHO POWER & LEN B. JORDAN

WHEN ISSUES ARE COMPLEX and controversial, they often devolve into whom the spokesperson for one side or the other is, and whether that individual radiates credibility. Advocates for either side can produce "indisputable facts," which are then disputed. A spokesperson that is articulate, intelligent, and has *gravitas* usually gains the upper hand.

Just such a person was Len B. Jordan. In 1940, after almost eight years of making a living running a sheep ranch in Hells Canyon. Jordan, his wife Grace and their three children moved into the town of Grangeville, the county seat for Idaho County. Geographically the largest county in Idaho, it is to this day sparsely settled. The county is larger than the state of Rhode Island, but much of the land is owned by the federal government and managed by the U.S. Forest Service. Additionally, the county contains two wilderness areas, the Gospel Hump and Mallard-Larkins, as well as a large part of the much larger Selway-Bitterroot Wilderness.

Jordan is one of the unsung heroes of Idaho history. He was never the kind to toot his own horn. He carefully chose his words and others listened. Jordan was born on May 15, 1899, in Mt. Pleasant, Utah (although not into an LDS family). His father, Leonard Eugene Jordan, was a county judge. His mother, Irene Beck Jordan, was a school teacher.

While quite young, the family relocated to Enterprise, Oregon. Jordan attended public school there and played football, graduating from Enterprise High School in 1917. As a 175-pound halfback, Jordan was fast

*Jordan Ranch house at Kirkwood Bar, "The Home Below Hells Canyon."
Photo: Steve Lee*

and strong. He worked on nearby ranches during the summers, as well as part-time during the school year. He attracted the attention of the University of Oregon football staff. He was offered and accepted a football scholarship.

Just the year before the "Webfoots" (the early nickname for the Ducks of today), coached by Hugo Bezdek, had gone undefeated (7-0-1, the lone blemish a tie with the University of Washington). The "Webfoots" eventually were given the win inasmuch as the Dawgs had used ineligible players.

On January 1, 1917, the Ducks won the third Rose Bowl, defeating a highly favored University of Pennsylvania team, 14 – 0. The Ducks would not win another Rose Bowl until 2012, a span of 95 years.

There is, however, another powerful attraction for young men – coming home a decorated war hero. The fact that the Ducks had changed coaches, hiring former Duck quarterback, Charles A. Huntington, might have

The Committee of Nine, Idaho Power & Len B. Jordan

The old bunkhouse, now a museum, at Kirkwood Bar. Photo: Steve Lee

had something to do with the decision also. Upon turning 18 in May of 1917, and shortly after graduating, Jordan enlisted in the United States Army.

He was commissioned a second lieutenant, but before he could be shipped overseas the Armistice ending the First World War was signed. Two years after enlisting, Jordan was given his honorable discharge. He returned to the University of Oregon, most likely because they renewed his football scholarship.

Jordan must have held his own but little is known about his football career inasmuch as records and summaries of the games Oregon played during the early 20s have been lost. We do know Jordan lettered his senior season in the fall of 1922 on a team that finished second in the old Pacific Coast Conference with a 6-1-1 record.

Suffice it to say, Jordan was never one to brag about his considerable accomplishments. He would probably, though, have been the first to tell you that his greatest accomplishment while at the university was capturing the heart and winning the hand of Grace Edgington.

Near as one can tell, theirs was a wonderful marriage in which each was deeply devoted to the other and their family. Though seven years older than her husband (Grace was born in Wasco, Oregon, on April 16, 1892), they met as classmates at the University of Oregon, and both graduated in 1923 Phi Beta Kappa from Oregon. Grace's degree was in English and she worked before her marriage as a journalist at the *Eugene Register-Guard* and the *Lewiston Morning Tribune*.

They married in Eugene on December 30, 1924, and embarked upon an adventure-filled life.

Grace took great pride in her writing skills and though being a homemaker was more than a full-time undertaking, she managed to find time to write. Her wonderful, slightly fictionalized account of their eight years running sheep in Hells Canyon, *Home Below Hells Canyon*, first published in 1954. Since then, it has gone through several reprintings and is the most widely read book about the canyon.

During the years her husband was governor (1950 to 1954) and then a United States senator (1962 to 1972) she often wrote columns about life in the capital cities that were carried by weekly and daily newspapers across Idaho. She also was an active member of the American Association of University Women.

In 1972 she published her last book, *The Unintentional Senator*, a personal biography covering many of the anecdotes and stories which derived from their years in Boise when her husband was governor to their ten years inside the Beltway when her husband served in the U.S. Senate. Chock full of astute insights and interesting observations, the book has been too easily dismissed as a compilation of some of her columns as well as some of Len's speeches. It is worth reading. Her basic decency and regard for her friends and neighbors as well as her optimism shone through. She was a tremendous asset to her husband throughout their life together.

Formal portrait of Grace Jordan, First Lady of Idaho and author of Home Below Hells Canyon. Photo: Boise State University archives

Despite the volatility of wool prices during the eight years the Jordans lived in the canyon, they were able to save enough for Len to establish several businesses in Grangeville – farm implements, autos, insurance and real estate. Like most who are raised in and around the ranching business, Jordan was a conservative Republican.

Active in local organizations that predominate in small towns across Idaho, such as the Chamber of Commerce, Elks, Shriners, and faithful attendance on Sunday at a church (the Jordans were Methodists), friends and colleagues urged him to run for the Idaho Legislature.

He succumbed to these blandishments, won the Republican nomination in the 1946 August primary and was elected to the State House from Idaho County in the Republican tide that swept the nation following World War II. Jordan defeated the Democrat, Shirlie Fenn, a well-regarded civic activist from Kooskia, a town on the Clearwater River in a canyon to the east of the Camas Prairie. Despite her popularity, Jordan won 1,970 to 1,317. Fenn became a loyal friend and supporter of the Jordan's within a few years.

Republican legislative leadership must have seen that here was someone ticketed for high office. Jordan was immediately placed on the three most important

House committees: appropriations, education and highways – an unheard of trifecta for a freshman.

That year (1946) also saw the first governor ever to be elected from northern Idaho, C.A. "Doc" Robins, a St. Maries physician and the state senator from Benewah County. Considered by most Idaho historians to be the first post-war, modern governor, Robins instituted much needed reforms, including the consolidation of over 1,200 school districts into some two hundred.

Jordan and Robins developed a liking for each other, in part because they saw the crying need of reforms in state government. However, as fiscal conservatives, they were committed to increasing revenues for better teacher's salaries and more support for education by a combination of program cuts and with economic expansion to generate the additional revenues needed.

In particular, each saw the critical need to revamp Idaho's antiquated highway system. Robins named Jordan to chair a Commission on Highway Reform, which with Jordan's strong guidance, produced an achievable blueprint for modernizing Idaho's highways and bridges. Some historians see Jordan's term as governor as an extension of the Robin administration.

Despite a solid record of accomplishments Jordan lost his re-election bid to his House seat. A well-liked farmer from Cottonwood, Joseph Kaschmitter, defeated Jordan in the 1948 election. Somewhat of a Democratic tide washed across the nation in reaction to the "do nothing" Congress. President Harry Truman ran successfully against that session of Congress in his campaign against Thomas Dewey. Kaschmitter captured 53.4% of the vote to Jordan's 46.6%. The Democrat served three terms and his last four years coincided with Jordan's four years as governor.

Some of the Jordan's friends felt Len had

been victimized by a "dirty trick." People came out of their churches the Sunday before the election to see windshields plastered with an unsigned charge saying that because Jordan supported Robin's massive consolidation of school districts school children in the county would no longer learn much. Balderdash that it was, enough folks believed it that Jordan lost the election.

Having been in Boise, however, brought some other hard-to-see benefits to the Jordans. Sometime during his term attorney, David Doane, originally from Grangeville and a recent graduate of the University of Idaho, introduced Jordan to a fraternity brother of his, an insurance business owner and devoted Republican named Bill Campbell. Campbell also was an avid sports fan and over the years owned interests in several professional Boise baseball teams. Shrewd, gifted, and decent he took a liking to Len Jordan. It was the beginning of a political alliance and friendship that would last their lifetimes.

Second, Jordan looked over the field of "wanna be" governor successors to Robins, who was limited to one four year term, and decided he could do a better job than anyone in the field.

Losing in 1948 was a blessing because it freed him to travel the state making his case to succeed Robins. With Campbell raising the money, writing speeches, drafting press releases (as did Grace) and providing the guidance and connections Jordan won the Republican primary in August, 1950 and then defeated the Democratic nominee, former State Auditor Cal Wright, by 14,000 votes, 52.6% (107,642 votes) to 47.4% (93,150 votes) in November.

Jordan's primary defeat of the other four Republicans – Reilly Atkinson, State Liquor Dispensary Director Seth Harper, former State Senator and Secretary of State J.D. Price and former State Representative and State Safety Commissioner George Vaughn surprised some, but the fact is he stood out in a field of rather bland aspirants. He was a good speaker and he radiated a cowboy charisma. Almost everywhere Jordan went, he found current or former legislators who liked and respected him. Many proudly became county chairs in Jordan's campaign.

Jordan also benefited from hiring a shrewd advertising person, Eddie Casebeer, who recognized that Jordan's craggy good looks and genuine soft-spoken manner radiated from a genuine rancher. Print and radio advertising emphasized Jordan's independence and ruggedness. It worked well.

Jordan won the Republican primary with a vote of 20,668. Atkinson, the former State Party chairman and a Boise businessman, ran second with 17,178 votes. Third place went to Price, who received 14,989 votes. Vaughn, was fourth with 5,418 votes and Harper came in last with 4,769 votes.

Former lieutenant governor and the first member of the LDS Church to serve as governor, Arnold Williams, expected to be the Democratic nominee. Voters though appeared displeased with the "job switch" Williams was a party to with Governor Charles Gossett in November 1945 after U.S. Senator John Thomas had died in office.

Gossett decided he wanted to be a senator. He resigned as governor which made Williams governor by succession and he turned around and named "citizen" Gossett to the vacant seat. Voters' memories were longer than the two expected. Both were turned out of office in 1946 with Williams losing to C.A. "Doc" Robins and Gossett losing to Henry Dworshak.

Williams lost the Democratic primary, however, to former three-term State Auditor Cal Wright, who captured more votes than anyone in either primary. Wright received 30,249 votes while Williams ran a distant second with 22,734 votes. George Hearsley, the head of the Idaho State Grange, had labor's endorsement but still lost badly, garnering just 11,564 votes.

For Wright it was sweet revenge. After becoming governor in 1945, besides naming Gossett to fill the vacant Senate seat, Williams also had to appoint a lieutenant governor to serve in his old job. He dangled the post in front of several different folks including Wright who then was residing in Wallace. Governor Williams invited Wright to come to Boise to discuss the office.

Governor Len B. Jordan on the day he hosted Dwight D. Eisenhower in Boise in 1952. Photo: BSU archives

When the meeting took place Williams chatted pleasantly about several subjects before ending the meeting, showing Wright the door and never mentioning the lieutenant governor's post. Wright understandably felt double-crossed and reminded Williams not too subtly of his belittling double-cross when the two talked shortly after the August primary. The exchange grew heated and relations were strained for several years thereafter.

The fall campaign between Jordan and Wright was a model of civility. Each demonstrated respect for the other. Each had a powerful behind-the-scenes patron: Jordan had Bill Campbell and Wright was backed by Tom Boise of Lewiston, a lobbyist who was considered the political boss of northern Idaho especially because he was the primary source of contributions to Democrat legislators.

During the primary Williams had been the source

of a whispering campaign that said Wright would be amenable to opening up Idaho to Nevada-style gaming and would loosen the liquor laws. Wright later told family and friends that while in Sun Valley during the general campaign he had been approached by folks representing gaming interests who offered to finance his campaign. To his credit he declined and when the election was over had to face a $9,000 debt which took him ten years to pay off.

While not accusing Wright of any connection with such interests, Jordan pledged to eliminate all forms of gaming then in existence in Idaho, from punch boards to the numerous slot machines across Idaho. Jordan also said he would toughen liquor laws. It is a safe guess that these items were well received in the Mormon counties of southeastern Idaho and contributed to Jordan's ultimate victory.

Undoubtedly, it was Campbell who introduced Jordan to the management of Idaho Power, the private utility that initially wanted to build the single high Hells Canyon dam rather than see the federal government build the dam utilizing the Bureau of Reclamation and the Army Corps of Engineers. It's a good guess also that Campbell was the one who introduced Jordan to some of the other behind-the-scenes players in Idaho political affairs – people like Larry Mills, a former House speaker who eventually headed up government affairs and did the lobbying for Boise-Cascade, a giant in the timber industry.

In addition, it's reasonable to speculate that Campbell introduced or sent letters of introduction for Jordan to folks like Logan Lanham who became the longest serving chief of government affairs for Idaho Power; Bob Paine, the Lewiston Area Manager for Washington Water Power; and its chief lobbyist Harry Wall, national committeeman for the Idaho Democrats; Tom Boise, the political boss of northern Idaho; and, Lloyd

Adams, an attorney in Rexburg who some consider to be the most influential lobbyist and non-elected politician Idaho ever produced.

The alliance of interests between Idaho Power and the Committee of Nine became apparent to Jordan immediately after the power company's change of heart. The utility wasn't so much interested in additional hydro-power resources at the time as it was in thwarting the effort of the remaining Roosevelt "New Dealers," especially those within the Bonneville Power Administration, to extend the reach of FDR and his "socialism" through the development of a newer, more modern version of Grand Coulee.

Few realize today that the proposed high Hells Canyon Dam would have been larger than Grand Coulee. Additionally, it would have been the cornerstone of a long-sought goal of the "News Dealers" to turn BPA into a Columbia Valley Authority (CVA) with power not just to market the hydroelectricity produced by Bureau of Reclamation and Army Corps of Engineers dams, but also, like the Tennessee Valley Authority (TVA), to build dams or nuclear plants and manage them.

This issue would play an important role in many of the federal races for the Congress from 1948 through 1964. It became one of those "telling" issues, i.e., it told the voter supposedly where the office seeker stood on the over-arching debate of the times: socialism vs. capitalism.

The year 1952 turned out to be a pivotal year for Governor Jordan. First, the Idaho Power Company, in a significant change of heart, announced it was no longer in the running to build the high Hells Canyon Dam. Instead, it announced it was going to file with the Federal Power Commission for approval to build three smaller dams on what is considered the Middle Snake. The three dams were Brownlee, Oxbow and Hells Canyon.

Even when he was in college at the University

of Oregon, Len Jordan displayed an unusual interest in water allocation and water law. He even wrote a senior paper on the subject. It is critical to understanding the future governor and senator that he accepted as the first inviolable principle of water law was "first in time, first in right."

Jordan intuitively understood that the three smaller dams would still allow for a pump-back operation, that is taking water which had passed through the three dams could be returned in a nice continued use cycle. This gave him an exit from the debate over whether the high dam would be a public or private project.

In effect, Idaho Power was withdrawing from the debate and Jordan would support the home-based utility. Jordan, however, was not about to give his support to Idaho Power without something in return. His condition stunned management of the utility. In exchange for his support, Jordan insisted the company agree in writing to subordinate the many downstream water rights to the upstream irrigation districts which were nine in number. Hence, the Committee of Nine.

Jordan had the utility by the proverbial cojones and so it had to agree. Idaho Power spent the next 50 years trying to renege on that agreement but it never succeeded. The Committee of Nine is one of the most powerful yet little known political entities in Idaho. The nine "water masters" of the federally built (by the Bureau of Reclamation within the Department of the Interior) and financed irrigation projects wield enormous influence southern Idaho.

All nine are members of the LDS Church, and any aspirant for high office in Idaho best understand and support the maintenance of Idaho water law. The key component is the phrase "First in time, first in Right."

Jordan reportedly believed this "pump-back" proposal would irrigate seven million more acres of farmland in southern Idaho, turning Idaho into a "super power" in production of more than potatoes and sugar beets. For Jordan the Snake River was the major artery, the blood, heart and soul that would serve in perpetuity. Without the water from the Salmon River being utilized, Corps and Bureau of Reclamation studies predicted that just an additional two million acres would be developed.

Having extracted his condition from the utility Len Jordan opposed any licensing of the major alternate sites in Hells Canyon: Pleasant Valley, High Mountain Sheep and Appaloosa. Jordan's interest in Snake River dams longs stood him in good stead. And the thesis he wrote in his graduate year, at Oregon, in which he proposed a series of dams be constructed along the Columbia and the Snake rivers to turn them into slack water to permit Lewiston to become the furthest inland seaport in the nation, was truly prescient.

It was also in 1952 that Governor Jordan met the president of Columbia University, former Supreme Commander of the Allied Forces in Europe Dwight D. Eisenhower. Jordan was hosting a meeting of the Western Governors Conference in Boise and invited the aspiring presidential candidate to drop by and visit, especially because all but one of the governors belonged to the Republican Party.

Eisenhower accepted the offer and flew into Boise for a brief visit. He received almost immediate visual reinforcement that there were many Americans waiting to vote him into the nation's highest office. All the way from the Boise airport to the Capitol, along Capitol Boulevard, the street was lined with people three and four deep, waiting to catch a glimpse of Ike and witness that dazzling smile.

While Ike's remarks were short and sweet, Jordan made hay with the future president and had a plethora of pictures ready to drop into newsletters and other communication materials that were put to good use ten years later. Campbell was one of those rare individuals who could see the horizon. He was always prepared.

To this day one can find those great pictures in different homes, galleries and studios across Idaho, as well as in what is now the Bunkhouse Museum at the old Jordan ranch at Kirkwood Bar.

Jordan's astute courting of Ike paid immediate dividends when he left the governorship. While Jordan was serving his one term supporters tried to get the Idaho Legislature to change the law to unlimited terms for state-wide officers.

Upon leaving office Jordan, accepted the post of chair of the U.S. delegation to the International Joint Boundary Commission (IJC), established by a 1909 treaty and approved by Congress as a bi-lateral commission with Canada, its purpose is to resolve disputes that arise along the almost 4,000 mile border that separates the two nations.

While not particularly well-known by the public, the IJC nonetheless has a critical role in negotiating power-sharing agreements, not the least of which is the US/Canadian pact on coordinated management of the dams along the Columbia River as well as the rest of the Columbia basin. A visitor to the Bonneville Power Administration's Operations Center is often surprised at the degree to which BPA, and its Canadian counterpart, British Columbia Hydro, operate on a remarkably integrated basis.

GAME-CHANGERS: GRACIE PFOST & BILL HAMILTON

THE YEAR 1952 also marked the arrival on the Idaho and national political scene of Gracie "Hell's Belle" Pfost, the first female to be elected to Congress from the state.

Born in a log cabin in Harrison, Arkansas, on March 12, 1906, she was one of five children. In 1911, the family moved "lock, stock and barrel" to Nampa where she received her basic education. In 1922, at the age of 16, she dropped out of Meridian High School to go to work as a milk analyst on a nearby dairy farm.

Her supervisor was Jack Pfost. Though twice her age, Jack and Gracie were smitten with each other and shortly thereafter they married. They were best friends, constant companions, and emotionally devoted to each other. They never had children.

While the 20s were called "roaring," for most folks in rural America life was a day-to-day struggle. Unbridled capitalism ruled supreme as more and more of the nation's wealth found its way into fewer and fewer hands. Gracie and Jack worked at a variety of jobs before Gracie attended and graduated from the Boise branch of the Links School of Business in 1929.

Mastering secretarial skills enabled Gracie to begin a 22-year career in the Canyon County Courthouse as deputy clerk-auditor-recorder before being elected to three terms as Canyon County Treasurer.

In the early 40s, she and Jack started a side business in real estate. Working in a county courthouse also necessitated more involvement in county politics and as she saw the growing need for government to be the assistant of last resort for the thousands of unemployed she grew more into the FDR Democrat she is known for being.

In 1950 she entered the race for the representative from the First Congressional District. She exuded energy and was an excellent campaigner. Some residents in Orofino and Priest River can still recall the time she entered the log-rolling contest during Lumberjack Days.

In the August primary, she defeated Harry Wall, a kind and courtly theater owner in Lewiston. Wall recovered from the loss and went on to a long and distinguished behind-the-scenes political career in Idaho Democratic politics. For many years, he was the national committeeman from Idaho. Candidates for the presidency through county commissioner sought his counsel.

In November, Pfost lost narrowly to the Republican nominee, John Wood, from Coeur d'Alene. Undeterred, she kept campaigning, in part because rumors were starting to circulate that former eight-term Congressman Comp White Sr. from Clark Fork was contemplating a run to regain the House seat he had held for sixteen years (1933-1947, 1949-1951).

Those rumors proved true. Undaunted and unfazed, Pfost defeated White in the primary and won a rematch, narrowly, against Wood in the fall and becoming the first woman ever to be elected to the Idaho congressional delegation.

She earned the sobriquet "Hells Belle" because of her vigorous support for the federal government to build a single high dam in Hells Canyon and market the "juice" through the Bonneville Power Administration. The Pacific Northwest Power Group still wanted private power to build and operate such projects. Even with the defection of Idaho Power, whose decision to license and build three smaller dams itself, had to have lessened the political heat in Idaho, Pfost's vigorous support never waned. She was a true "New Deal" Democrat who revered FDR.

In 1956, Pfost was part of another political first – this one was national.

Republicans nominated for the First District seat a Coeur d'Alene journalist, Louise Shadduck, who came to the race with political savvy and experience having served as chief of staff to Governor C.A. "Doc" Robins and then became the first woman head of a state agency when Robert Smylie was governor.

Shadduck had set up and run the first department of commerce and tourism for the state of Idaho. The challenge by Shadduck to wrest the office away from Pfost was the first time in the nation's 180-year history that the two major parties had a woman as their standard-bearer.

First District Congresswoman "Hell's Belle," Gracie Pfost. An ardent supporter of the Federal government building one high dam in the canyon she served 10 years, 1952 to 1962. Photo: BSU archives

Both were excellent campaigners who understood the retail nature of Idaho politics. People in Idaho expected to see their federal office-holders, shake their hands, and look 'em in the eye. They campaigned up, down and across the First District. It was also a presidential election year with a popular candidate, Dwight D. Eisenhower, at the top of the ticket. This meant that probabilities were high there would be a high vote turnout. There was, but it largely favored the Democrats.

A young Boise attorney, Frank Church, defeated the incumbent Republican Senator Herman Welker, "Little Joe from Idaho," as he was dubbed by detractors who deplored his throwing in with the communist-baiting Wisconsin Senator Joe McCarthy.

Republican congressional candidate Louise Shadduck. Her 1956 challenge of Pfost was the first time in U.S. History that each major party nominated a woman to contest a seat in Congress. Courtesy: Boise State University archives.

Incumbents, unless they have really screwed up, are hard to beat. Such was the case with Gracie Pfost. First District voters were starting to feel more comfortable with her and saw little need to change. Pfost turned aside Shadduck's challenge easily, defeating her 60,170 to 48,174.

To the surprise of many, Schadduck never again sought public office, disappointing many who thought she would be the one to break the glass ceiling above the governor's chair or a seat in the U.S. Senate.

While a Hells Canyon debate between the two might logically have taken place there is no existing record that it did. By the late 50s other players were walking onto the Hells Canyon stage, and most of them were starting to coalesce around the idea that there should be no dams in the geologically and culturally unique canyon.

Len Jordan's service on the International Joint Boundary Commission furthered his water expertise credentials and negotiating skills, and as the years passed he garnered more accolades for his ability to skillfully defend U.S. interests from the Columbia to the St. Lawrence Seaway.

With 20/20 hindsight, it appears inevitable that Pfost and Jordan would appear opposite each other on an Idaho ballot. With the death of Senator Henry Dworshak on July 23, 1962, the die was cast. Whether Governor Smylie first called Governor Jordan to offer him the appointment or Governor Jordan called Governor Smylie and asked for the appointment is the subject of debate.

Under Idaho law, whoever received the appointment still had to stand for voter ratification at the next general election. Smylie's nomination of Jordan was well received and most political observers expected Rep. Pfost to be the Democratic nominee. Both held the other in high regard so the campaign was civil with few fireworks and a focus on the issues. Again, there is little in the record to indicate that the future of Hells Canyon was discussed or debated.

It turned out to be a close election, Jordan prevailed by fewer than 5,000 votes.

After the election, Pfost accepted a political appointment from the Kennedy Administration to a sub-cabinet post. Pfost died suddenly and unexpectedly shortly after checking into Baltimore's prestigious John Hopkins University Hospital.

Len Jordan, on the other hand, would serve 10 years in the U.S. Senate and play a critical role in Hells Canyon.

In the early 50s, not only was 1952 a significant year in Idaho, so was 1954, especially for those in and around Lewiston who were aware what a natural wonder Hells

Canyon is and how criminal it would be to fill it with a gigantic slack-water reservoir.

The butterfly effect of an event over half a world away was about to change the political calculus of the canyon. Almost overnight, hundreds and then thousands, of people who previously had not been able to visit Hells Canyon were provided a way to do so.

The "enabler" was the development of the jet boat by an Englishman living in New Zealand. The Hells Canyon "Hall of Heroes" starts with Sir William Hamilton and his invention.

New Zealand, especially the South Island, is as beautiful as mountainous Idaho. New Zealand abounds with many rivers and streams, which, like many in Idaho, run shallow most of the summer.

New Zealanders needed a watercraft that could skim on top of the water. Hamilton thought about it and saw an analogy to the modern jet engine that sucks in air, mixes it with jet fuel, controls the explosion and creates forward thrust. He felt the principle could work well with water. The thrust forward had to lift the boat and the weight of a powerful engine.

Initial plans were drawn utilizing wood and steel, but the weight proved to be a problem, creating a deep enough draft that conventional outboards did not have enough power to lift the craft on top of the waves moving along at a speed sufficient to "plane" the boat.

The answer proved to be easier than expected: lighter material for the hull of the craft, especially molded light aluminum and a car engine, which despite its weight, gave more than sufficient power to get the boat hydroplaning. While this was well before the Internet, word-of-mouth spread the news.

A "cottage industry" sprung up around Lewiston, with small shops creating jet boats from small to large. The real winner was Hells Canyon, as more and more

Game-Changers: Gracie Pfost & Bill Hamilton

Large jet boat like that used by operators of one day tours from Lewiston/Clarkston into Hells Canyon with a noon stop at Kirkwood Bar. Photo: Steve Lee

people now had ready access. Additionally, part of the travel package offered by companies that ran cruises from Portland up the Columbia added a jet boat trip into Hells Canyon.

Just above the confluence of the Snake and the Salmon, tour company operators would slow their boat and point back down the canyon to a white marker that indicated where the top of the reservoir behind the once-proposed high Hells Canyon Dam would have been.

The narration always draws words of anger and outrage.

Jet boat access generated the critical mass of public support necessary to stop a major effort by the federal government to get back into the dam-building business. Too many people were witnessing with their own eyes the splendor of Hells Canyon.

THE HELLS CANYON PRESERVATION COUNCIL

BROCK EVANS' CONCLUSIVE WORK on securing protection for Hells Canyon was the culmination of the work of hundreds of others, many of whom labored in anonymity. They laid the ground work before he arrived. Evans would be the first to acknowledge the value of this the scene-setting work as he took a local issue and turned it into a national cause.

Three of the earlier staunch supporters for protecting Hells Canyon were Dick Rivers, Floyd Harvey and Russ Mager. In much the same way that Brock Evans was captured by the stark beauty of this special place, these three instinctively knew there was something magical about Hells Canyon.

Harvey has the distinction of being one of two individuals who enticed Brock Evans into "hell." Harvey, and Dick Rivers, who ran the weekly boat that delivered mail and other goods to the remote ranches up and down the canyon, share the credit. Besides delivering the mail, his manifest sometimes included a few passengers who paid for passage in and out of the canyon.

Harvey also maintained a lodge for hunting and fishing guests at Willow Creek, some 60 miles upstream from Lewiston. Upon learning that the private power consortium was planning to license and build the High Mountain Sheep dam he became a one-man crusader vowing to fight the dam as long as he had breath to breathe.

Many saw him as a latter-day Don Quixote tilting at windmills, an out-of-step, "dwelling in the past" knight errant. He targeted organizations he thought would

Jet boat heading downriver as seen from Suicide Point. Photo: Steve Lee

be allies, such as the Idaho Fish & Game Department, the Wildlife Federation and the Lewiston Chamber of Commerce. All rebuffed him.

Serendipitously, Harvey contacted the newly anointed northwest representative for the Sierra Club, a young attorney, Brock Evans, who immediately invited Harvey to bring his "dog and pony," show to the Seattle area for the club's next executive committee meeting. The executive committee often met at the home of Polly Dyer, a long-time, stalwart supporter of the Sierra Club. This particular time, they met in Emily Haig's home on Hood Canal.

By any measure, Harvey's trip was a success. According to Evans, the committee was impressed by Harvey's photos and story. The committee authorized Evans to find time in his calendar to look into the issue and to come back with a recommendation.

Evans quickly made plans to journey into the canyon by September to get his own take. He undertook other moves that proved to be far-sighted and propitious, too: He wrote to the U.S. Supreme Court asking for intervention status in a key lawsuit the court was reviewing and, he recognized the need for a local organized group opposing dam building in the canyon.

"I believe if enough local sportsmen and others express their concerns in an organized way about this project, there may be a chance to do something about it," Evans said at the time. The Idaho Alpine Club stepped up to the plate.

Russ Mager hosted the organizational meeting at his Lewiston home July 19, 1967, for what morphed into the Hells Canyon Preservation Council. It would become a indispensible support group to the efforts orchestrated by Evans. The core of the Idaho Alpine Club were professionals who worked at the Idaho National Laboratory, one of several nuclear energy labs maintained by the U.S. Department of Energy near Idaho Falls.

"Crusaders" present at the birth of the HCPC included Boyd Norton, Jerry Jayne, Paul Fritz, Al MGlinsky, Cyril Slansky, James Campbell, Floyd Harvey and, of course, Russ Mager, who became the HCPC's first president, Jayne was elected the first vice president.

In September 1967, Evans, along with Jayne Campbell and Cliff Merritt of the Wilderness Society, took Harvey's jet boat up to his lodge at Willow Creek. The next day he took them another 12 miles to where Granite Creek flows into the Snake.

It was on this trip that Evans began to focus on the fact that it was not enough to oppose the High Mountain Sheep Dam. Some instrument had to be put in place that would ensure permanent protection of the canyon. Evans knew protective legislation had to be drafted and enacted quickly.

Brock Evans, then the regional director for the Sierra Club and the catalyst for the creation of the Hells Canyon NRA. Photo: Brock Evans

Though a relative newcomer to the contact sport of politics, Evans knew that once he had drawn up the legislation to protect Hells Canyon he had to find a champion in either the House or the Senate to sponsor and shepherd the bill through a complicated process of hearings, committee meetings, agency reviews and a final sign off by the President.

Back in Seattle, while drafting his version of the preferred legislation, Evans realized he faced a serious challenge in finding a sponsor. Congressional protocol dictated that one of the two House members in whose district the proposed NRA was located, if not a primary sponsor, had to show tacit approval by serving as a co-sponsor.

On the Idaho side of the river, Evans was looking at freshman Congressman James A. McClure, a newly elected conservative Republican.

Evans wasn't sure where McClure stood on the issue of protecting the river and banning any further dam building in the canyon. He did know, though, that McClure had previously hiked the canyon and the Seven

Devils area. Evans hoped the canyon had worked its magic on McClure, but knew he could not rely on that. Further tempering his view of the canyon and a future dam was the strong support Idaho Power Company gave McClure's campaign.

On the Oregon side, however, Evans had a potential champion: Second District Congressman Al Ullman, from Baker City. Ullman, elected in 1956 as a moderate Democrat, was considered a rising star by his fellow caucus members.

Further fueling Evans' optimism was the fact that in Ullman's first successful congressional campaign he had been a proponent for the federal government to build one high dam in the canyon. The issue had proven to be a major factor in his victory and he had carefully followed up.

Ullman attended Whitman College in Walla Walla, Washington. Following his graduation, he taught at Port Angeles High School, then moved to eastern Oregon.

A federally constructed dam as opposed to a privately constructed one was still a raging debate. Elections in the impacted areas affirmed the private sector as the favored builder. In checking with others, Evans was warned about Ullman. Some had divined that he harbored higher ambitions. Sponsoring or even co-sponsoring unpopular legislation could torpedo Ullman's ambitions.

Ullman was hell bent on becoming chairman of the powerful House Ways and Means Committee and he was careful not to antagonize any of the old bulls who controlled the House and Senate in the late 50s.

His patience paid off. Ullman was elevated to the chairmanship in 1973, and selected as the permanent chairman in 1975, a position he competently filled until defeated in his re-election campaign of 1980. Evans was wise not to have sought him as his bill's champion early on.

Ullman "came late" to the party, introducing a bill of his own in 1971 that would have established a modest Hells Canyon NRA. But the measure did not explicitly rule out dams and thus garnered little support. It is fair to say that once Ullman became chair of Ways and Means he became a strong ally and supporter of the bill protecting the canyon and the river.

The chairmanship was ultimately the cause of Ullman's stunning defeat in 1980. He made the classic mistake of not regularly returning to his district, thinking that news clips, radio and television reports, and occasional in-district speeches would be enough because constituents in his district just had to know what an important person he was in D.C.

Republican Denny Smith defeated the 24-year incumbent, according to official records, but in reality one newspaper ad that ran in all the weeklies and dailies in Oregon's Second District was the reason. It was a simple, but effective ad, headlined: "This is Your Congressman's District Home." The picture was Ullman's post office box in the Baker Post Office. Smith's campaign found out that Ullman sold his house and owned no property in the district he was representing. It ended his career.

Evans gave serious consideration to either one of the state of Washington's two powerful senators, Warren G. "Maggie" Magnuson or Henry Jackson (called "Scoop" by friends). Jackson was chair of one of the germane committees, Interior and Insular Affairs, although the chairman did not often sponsor bills which would impact them. Magnuson was chair of the Commerce Committee. Evans would need the support of "The Gold Dust" twins, but he recognized they could not carry the legislation.

Evans also gave thought to a sophomore congressman from Spokane, Tom Foley, whose district barely touched the canyon but overall much of the district's income depended on a reliable transportation system to get its wheat and other ag products to market. Foley's constituents were supportive of dams in the Columbia Basin, but an historic distrust of government had a solid majority favoring private power over public power. Completion of Idaho Power's Hells Canyon Dam in 1968 and completion of Lower Monumental Dam in 1973 enabled Lewiston to become the nation's furthest inland seaport which provided a cheap way for shipping grain to the coast by barge rather than by train or truck.

It further ensured wheat farmers the lowest cost for getting their products to ports and terminals on the northwest's coast – ports with terminals like Bellingham, Everett, Seattle, Tacoma and Portland, all of which were one to two days closer to the profitable Asian market than the California ports.

Those with the most interest and the most at stake were Idaho's two senators, Frank Church, the Democrat and Len B. Jordan, the Republican.

When the issue of dams first surfaced, Church initially was supportive of one "high" dam to be constructed by the federal government at the Pleasant Valley site. Jordan supported the same site, but wanted it built by the private sector. Each showed great deference to the other and kept one another informed. Both were sincere devotees of the so-called "no surprises" rule. Each had reservations as they started to hear from their constituents.

Eventually, in 1968, the two introduced legislation to suspend all studies on dams in Hells Canyon and its suitability for dams for ten years. Once again, Evans' instincts were correct.

Looking back at Oregon, Evans thought he saw a glimmer of hope that Ullman might choose to be his champion. It was not in the cards. Evans' meeting with Oregon Senator Mark Hatfield also didn't go well. The two didn't hit it off; he found Hatfield self-righteous and "a prissy."

This contrasted sharply with the meeting he had with Oregon's other senator, the newly elected Bob Packwood, who had upset the maverick former University of Oregon Law School dean, Wayne Morse, by 3,500 votes in the 1968 election. Evans and Packwood hit it off. Evans knew personal compatibility would be critical in the months and years ahead.

Packwood did, however, possess major shortcomings. He rubbed many of his colleagues the wrong way. He had a prickly personality, was not viewed as a team player, and emoted pure, raw ambition. One of his more serious problems was a failure as a freshman to keep his mouth shut and to show deference to his seniors. Packwood seemed incapable of appreciating seniority.

Some felt Evans had committed a terrible tactical mistake in not lobbying Church and/or Jordan more diligently to be the champion. Evans, however, could point to the smooth way he and his cohorts were able to work effectively with Packwood and his staff.

Despite Packwood's later fall from grace, Evans never apologized nor repent for using the one advocate he initially could find among the 535 members of the Congress. Messages and lessons are often conveyed in imperfect vessels.

For Evans, the biggest mystery was James Albertus McClure, the freshman congressman from Idaho's First Congressional District. He was viewed as an ideological, right-winger and had been an early advocate of the Liberty Amendment which would have sold off to the highest bidder choice parcels of federal land, busted up "oppressive federal agencies" and left the federal government doing nothing more than delivering the mail and defending our shores.

Yet Evans was also picking up reports that McClure

was more practical than ideological, that he studied the issues and reached conclusions not always driven by ideology but more on their merits. McClure was solution-oriented, had a wry sense of humor, and could laugh at himself.

Evans decided to do a bit more digging into McClure's background and confessed to being surprised at what he found.

He discovered McClure had not taken a firm stand on whether there should be dams in Hells Canyon, despite Idaho Power being a major contributor. From a philosophical standpoint, it was safe to assume that if another Grand Coulee-like dam were to be built in the canyon, McClure would have opted for a private company to build the project, especially because a private company would have to pay taxes.

First, however, the threshold decision had to be made. What Evans quickly saw was McClure did not lack opinions. It was easy to find examples where McClure would take a stand in defense of conserving and protecting upstream water rights. McClure would pontificate about the importance of being on guard against sneaky Californians who were coveting Idaho's water. Every Idahoan walking would support that stance, especially the former governor and about to retire Senator Jordan.

Once in the Senate, McClure began to unveil his privately held view that Hells Canyon was truly unique and should be given some form of federal protection. Evans discovered that McClure had gone backpacking in and around the Seven Devils Mountains that hover above the canyon.

He heard how McClure enjoyed telling the story of when they lived in Council and his father, a local attorney, had hiked deep into the canyon to meet a client. Hells Canyon had a special place in his heart, and when the time came for someone to shepherd the Hells Canyon National Recreation Area bill through the Senate and House, Evans found himself confronted with the two "work horses," Jim McClure and Frank Church, as opposed to the "show horse," Bob Packwood.

Much to Evans' surprise, at the end of the day it was McClure and Church who delivered the bill to President Gerald Ford for signing.

Even *The Lewiston Morning Tribune*, which seldom had anything good to write about McClure, gave him a "cheer" and applauded his key role in securing passage of the NRA law.

In a laudatory editorial on December 21, 1975, the Tribune wrote:

> *"Twenty years in the making, the Hells Canyon Recreation Area will become a reality upon the signature of President Ford. Approved by Congress Friday, the bill essentially preserves the free-flowing status of the Middle Snake River south of Lewiston...Credits for establishing a recreation area for Hells Canyon must go, of course, to early day environmentalists whose foresight delayed further power company designs on the already concrete-choked Snake River. Back pats must also be given to members of Congress from the northwest, like Representative Al Ullman, Senator Robert Packwood, and Senator Frank Church, who were behind the legislation from the start.*
>
> *"But the highest tribute should be reserved for Idaho Senator James McClure, whose pro-recreation area stand placed him at odds with many of his fellow conservatives, and those segments of industry from whom he receives much of his campain support. McClure led the Senate passage and helped to overcome House opposition, championed mainly by his fellow Republican from Idaho,*

Rep. Steve Symms. McClure steadfastly held out, however uncomfortable, against pressure from political allies to soften his stance.

"McClure placed the welfare of future generations over political expediency. For that, he deserves recognition. A gold Star for Jim McClure."

Others might term it an Idaho example of profiles in courage.

McClure's forthright stance ended up being of great value to Church whose aide, Mike Wetherall, drafted the final bill. When Jordan announced his retirement in August 1971, he and Church had long ago taken the ball away from Evans' champion, Senator Packwood, and in 1971 the two Idaho senators rammed through the Senate their 1968 bill declaring a now seven-year moratorium on any dam building in the canyon or any studies on the subject.

The beauty in this measure was it gave Evans and his fellow anti-dam conservationists more time to create a critical mass of national public support. It turned out Evans only needed four of the seven years.

With 20/20 historical hindsight, one of the pleasures for conservationists and Idaho historians is seeing Church's position evolve and tilt to the environmental side of the debate. Initially, there were flags of concern within the Idaho conservation community. In the dispute over whether the dam should be federally or privately built, Church adopted the orthodox Democratic position that new dams should be built and owned by Uncle Sam.

The issue of whether to outright ban future dams on the Snake, however, was a different matter. In 1956, Idaho Power fiercely opposed Church's election on the fact that he wanted public ownership for the dams.

Church, thus, had to weigh carefully how far he would go publicly and whether he could maintain a public stance of ambiguity, especially in light of Idaho Power still having Brownlee and Hells Canyon dams to complete above the Hells Canyon gorge.

Further temporizing his dam stance was that the Army Corps of Engineers wasn't scheduled to finish its work on Lower Granite dam until 1974, the final link in making Lewiston a "seaport." Every political officeholder in Idaho paid lip service to the virtues of these dams above and below the main gorge. Church wisely bit his tongue and bidded his time.

While Evans was busy composing a draft bill in the waning months of 1967, he also began planning numerous trips to Idaho in 1968 to meet leaders of local and statewide conservation organizations. He wanted to start building that critical mass of local public support he knew would be the catalyst for success at the national level.

He was not laboring alone. By this time, several organizations and local groups, as well as more than a few private citizens, were weighing in on the members of their congressional delegations and key officials in the Johnson Administration.

For example, four members of the Idaho Alpine Club, a group comprised largely of the scientists and engineers who worked at the then-named National Reactor Testing Station in the desert 60 miles west of Idaho Falls, became converts to the Hells Canyon protection cause following the viewing of Russ Mager's slide show. The four were Boyd Norton, Jerry Jayne, Al McGlinsky and Dick Wilde.

They became key agitators/advocates in the Hells Canyon Preservation Council.

Mager, also in April, wrote to one of Evans' nominal bosses, Sanford Stepfer, the Sierra Club's Pacific Northwest regional chapter chairman, seeking a formal statement of opposition to any dam in Hells Canyon. Stepfer's response was in keeping with the strategy on which Evans had embarked, one of building a critical mass of opposition at the local level that would be the catalyst for making the matter a national issue.

The nascent effort received a tremendous and unexpected boost when on June 5, 1967, the U.S. Supreme Court, on a 6-2 vote, vacated the license for the proposed High Mountain Sheep Dam. In the opinion written for the majority, Associate Justice William O. Douglas, directed the issue back to the Federal Power Commission with instructions to reopen the hearing process.

Justice Douglas opined that the test of whether the dam was in the public interest had to include a thorough examination of alternatives including an examination of the "no dam" option. Douglas also specifically mandated there be an examination on the impact of the dam on the salmon and steelhead runs.

The court opened the possibility that "the best dam for Hells Canyon might be no dam at all. The test," wrote Douglas, "is not solely whether the region will be able to use the electric power." The test is whether the project will be in the public interest. And that determination can be made only after an exploration of all issues relevant to the "public interest," including future power demand and supply, alternate sources of power, the public interest in preserving reaches of wild rivers and wilderness areas, the preservation of anadromous fish for commercial and recreational purposes, and the protection of wildlife."

Evans recognized that the unexpected "gift" from the high court was just a stay of execution and would bring a new trial. This led him to the aforementioned letter to the Supreme Court asking if there could now be intervenors including, his entrance on behalf of the Sierra Club and the Federation of Western Outdoor Clubs. While his formal petition to intervene was strenuously opposed by attorneys for the dam, the court granted Evans permission to intervene.

Shortly after the ruling made the news (he was reading a back issue of the *Lewiston Tribune* one afternoon in his office and saw a small item noting the decision), Evans wrote Mager asking for a local group of some sort to join the request for intervention and then to become a party to whatever legal course they pursued.

In his letter to Mager, Evans said he thought that if enough local sportsmen and others, in an organized manner, made known their opposition, something could be done. The logical group was the Idaho Alpine Club, but it soon became clear that the organization should morph into a new group with protection of Hells Canyon being the clear mission. And in July the Hells Canyon Preservation Council was formed.

In September, the FPC granted intervenor status to Evans on behalf of the groups he represented, and other groups, including the Idaho Water Resources Board. Anyone familiar with Idaho water law and history knew this was a protective move by the Committee of Nine still intent on preserving the option for a pump back dam.

With Evans poking sticks and members of the HCPC starting to target friends and neighbors, things began to snowball for dam opponents. The HCPC put out its first newsletter later in the fall explaining its mission. It also solicited other groups to join the cause. Much to Evans' delight the response was heart-warming.

The Idaho Wildlife Federation, despite the reluctance of its chair, Bruce Bowler, joined, as did the Idaho Outfitters and Guides Association, the North Idaho Wilderness Committee and the Oregon Fish and Game Council. Almost as important was Don Thomas' success in getting the Lewiston Chamber of Commerce to withdraw its support for the High Mountain Sheep dam.

Cyril Slansky prepared a detailed report and slide

show outlining the case against High Mountain Sheep, and other dams in the canyon. He began attending conservation group meetings and conferences around the region to present his program. Part of the brilliance was not just the environmental case against a dam. He also rendered a compelling economic case against dams.

    The HCPC scored an additional coup when in the early spring of 1968, Bill Blair, a prize-winning reporter on environmental affairs for *The New York Times*, accepted an invitation to see for himself what the issues were. In April, Blair tagged along on a trip through the canyon, a three-night excursion with Jerry Jayne, Boyd Norton, and James Campbell.

    Once again, Floyd Harvey was johnny-on-the-spot, providing most of the transportation and the lodging. Erring on the side of caution since it was spring and the water flow was high, Harvey took the group two at a time through the largest rapids. While traversing the Sluice Creek Rapids, Harvey had his boat's front windshield shatter.

    On returning from Hells Canyon, Blair wrote two stories that appeared in the June 2, 1968, edition of *The Times*. A week later the *The Times* editorialized in favor of protecting the canyon.

    Evans was ecstatic. It proved to be the harbinger of numerous news stories across the nation endorsing protection for canyon and gorge.

Looking upriver at Big Bar from Suicide Point. Photo: Steve Lee

BROCK EVANS TO THE RESCUE

FOR THOSE THAT BUILD DAMS and for those who see them as fishkillers, the date of June 5, has special meaning and it has nothing to do with D-Day. Two "game changing" events with consequences, some unintended, occurred for Hells Canyon.

On that day, as noted earlier, the United States Supreme Court vacated a Federal Power Commission license to build a dam in Hells Canyon, and ordered the agency to conduct a more thorough public review.

On June 5, 1976, in a far-off corner of southeastern Idaho the newly constructed Teton Dam failed, killing eleven people and leaving hundreds homeless. Both events would have repercussions in the debate over dams in Hells Canyon.

When it comes to passing out the accolades for the salvation and preservation of Hells Canyon, one person stands above all others, the truly indispensable one, Brock Evans.

Born on May 24, 1937, into a middle-class family in Columbus, Ohio, to Adele Walley and Ray Evans, Jr.

His father, and grandfather, Ray Evans, Jr., and Ray Evans Sr., were editorial cartoonists at the *Columbus Dispatch*. At an early age Evans was drawn into political and policy discussions around the dinner table. It helped to hone his debating skill and love of history. Not surprisingly, Evans imbibed the father and grandfather's conservative Republican view of the world which pervaded (and still does) the Columbus milieu. His mother's sisters were all liberal Catholic social workers, but his father's strong and articulate views dominated the household and dinnertime discussions.

Evans says he hardly knew any Democrats while growing up. It wasn't until he was in law school at the University of Michigan that two events forced a reassessment of his thinking. The first was a 2 a.m. whistle-stop train visit by Senator John F. Kennedy during the 1960 presidential race which Evans attended out of curiosity (he still voted for Richard Nixon). The second, he fell in love with a liberal, Jewish undergraduate, Rachel Cohen, from Lynn, Massachusetts.

By 1964, however, Evans completed his conversion to the Democratic side of the ledger. The Republican nomination of Arizona Senator Barry Goldwater for president pushed him over the edge.

Evans began his schooling at Main-Montrose Elementary School in Bexley, Ohio, a suburb of Columbus which was viewed by others as one of the poorer parts of Bexley. By the time Evans entered the 8th grade, the family had moved to Upper Arlington, a more upscale neighborhood in northwest Columbus and Evans attended Junior-Senior Upper Arlington High School.

It was becoming evident to Evans' father, Ray, that his son was unusually bright. Ray Evans' epiphany came on the day he found his son with his Russian coin collection, thumbing through a Cyrillic dictionary. Evans was fifteen at the time and had for several years been collecting old U.S. coins and then ancient and medieval coins – an curiosity that grew out of his interest in history.

Like many young people in middle class families after World War II, Evans was expected, once a teenager, to find summer work and contribute to the family treasury. At fourteen, he peddled an ice cream wagon during the summer.

During his fifteenth and sixteenth years he was a newspaper carrier. A school chum introduced Evans to coin collecting and Evans subscribed to catalogs, eventually winning some coin bids. By the time he was fifteen, he had acquired an impressive collection but was frustrated because he couldn't read the inscriptions. Hence, the Cyrillic dictionary.

 It finally clicked with his father that his son was in the wrong school; public high school was doing nothing for his son. He wanted to enroll him into a more demanding and challenging private school. It was one of those rare moments when one's life is irrevocably changed. Ray arranged for his son to attend the exclusive Columbus Academy. There were only 25 boys in each class and no girls to distract them. In fall of 1952, Brock enrolled in the sophomore class.

 The school was expensive, but Evans was able to get a scholarship. Students were taught to address their teachers as "sir." There was a dress code.

 One of the things Evans liked best about the school was the respect for being smart and earning good grades. In public school students had to hide their smarts for fear of being ostracized. "At the Academy, 20 out of 25 students are striving and doing the work. It's a challenging competitive environment," Evans said. "In the public school I would venture to guess the numbers are reversed – only five of the 25 are striving – the rest are goof offs, a distraction to learning and attending school because it's a glorified baby sitting institution."

 Evans deemed his time at Columbus Academy a "powerful experience." He loved an atmosphere that respected learning and took great delight in being able to play football in an environment that did not worship athletes or categorize them as "dumb jocks." On offense he played the "blindside" tackle position with his prime responsibility being to protect the quarterback from being tackled.

 Evans also played the critical middle linebacker

position when the Academy was on defense.

"I was always slow," Evan's recalls, "but big enough to block my assignment when we had the ball and tackle the opponent when playing defense."

More than anything, Evans credits the Academy with expanding his horizons and learning about the rest of the world. When it came time to send out college applications, Evans became family apostate of sorts when he declared he was not going to attend Ohio State.

He ended up applying to six schools: Harvard, Princeton, Conneticut Weslyan, Williams, Ohio Weslyan, and Denison. He was accepted by all six, which presented him with another fork in life's road.

He narrowed his choices to the two Ivy League schools, Harvard and Princeton, then settled on the latter.

Evans said the key difference between the two was the alumni he knew. "The real men I knew and admired most – especially my football coach, Jack White – were Princeton alumni, while the Harvard alums were not as impressive to me."

Evans also modestly mentions he aced the SAT test with a perfect score of 800 in the general language arts and math. Evans attributes much of his later life success to his years at Princeton.

Following his graduation in June 1959, and in spite of his acceptance by the University of Michigan Law School, Evans began searching for a job on a sea-going vessel that would enable him to satisfy his yearning to experience the world.

He landed a job as a "maskingut" (engine boy) on a Norwegian ship, the MS *Capto*, a tramp steamer headed for India via the Suez Canal and back by way of South Africa. He spent four months at sea and loved every minute of it.

As he was returning home from his sea adventure he received greetings from Uncle Sam informing him that he was needed by his country. The pink draft notice came in

Brock Evans to the Rescue

the mail, so Evans decided rather than be drafted he would enlist in the Marines.

The decision was another of those life-changing experiences. "The Marines do a superb job of instilling in one a sense of discipline, the importance of good planning and timely execution," he said, "The Marines enabled me to multi-task while staying focused."

Following graduation from the Michigan Law School, Evans heard his own "call of the wild" and headed West to put down a tap root in the Seattle area. Being an Ivy League graduate with impressive marks from the University of Michigan Law School made it easy for him to get on with an established law firm. He soon discovered the art of billing a client every possible dime and churning away resolving client problems just was not his cup of tea.

In the spring of 1967, Evans left his practice in Seattle to accept a new position as Northwest representative of the Sierra Club – the only paid, full-time conservationist position north of Los Angeles. His "territory" was most of the West as well as Alaska and western Canada.

Evans says he heard of Hells Canyon for the first time in 1966. By a strange turn of fate, the law firm he worked for at the time had as its major client the Washington Public Power Supply System – a consortium of the mostly large customers of the Bonneville Power (BPA). BPA is the federally established agency that markets the electricity produced from the public dams built on the Columbia and Snake River systems.

At the time Evans left, there was a petition sitting before the Federal Energy and Regulatory Commission (FERC) from the Pacific Northwest Power Company (PNPC), a combine of private power companies, to build a "high" dam in Hells Canyon, flooding the last 120 miles of its inner gorge. Evans was asked by a senior partner to work up a brief.

Say no more. In 1966 Evans could have been launched

on a different path that would still have brought him fame, if not fortune. At the time, he declined to write that brief, but he had little idea how critical his role would be in the upcoming fight to protect Hells Canyon once he began his work with the Sierra Club.

A brief before the Supreme Court is every young lawyer's dream. Evans hated dams – the whole idea of dams – and thought he could not objectively present his brief. Even though Marc Reisner's great book, *Cadillac Desert*, was 20 years in the future, Evans would have subscribed to every word of Reisner's masterful analysis on why most dams were due to predictable failure. Evans begged off, wanting no part of what he saw as a dirty business.

Destiny was calling and it is not easily denied. A year later, on a May morning in 1967 at Evans' first regional executive committee meeting, from out of the heart of "darkest Idaho," came a visitor – Floyd Harvey of Lewiston. Harvey, a long time boatman and guide in Hells Canyon, loved the canyon and the mighty Snake River that had carved the gorge. He knew every bend, cove and cliff. His eloquence and passion about the subject resonated with all who listened.

The Executive committee directed Evans to do what he could to stop future dams in Hells Canyon.

With misgivings that anything could be done at such a late date, Evans started his research. The license had been already granted, and the only issue before the Supreme Court was about who won the "privilege" to desecrate Hells Canyon. Evans says he was morose and unhappy about the assignment for weeks. He confesses he could come up with no solution to the challenge, especially in light of the Sierra Club's limited resources at the time. That's when the first of several miracles occurred. Saviors can be recipients of miracles as well as producers. The miracle took place in the venue least expected – the United States Supreme Court.

To Evans' credit he realized they had a brief opening

and a fighting chance to change the entire nature of the Hells Canyon battle.

Justice William O. Douglas wrote: "The Court will not now make a decision on *who* gets to build this dam. The first question that must be answered is *whether* there should be any dam at all. Therefore, we remand this case back to the FPC for a determination on this one point: should there be a dam or not." The words themselves amounted to a stunning legal precedent; never before had the Supreme Court – *any* court – ever questioned the 'common wisdom' of building a dam.

Evans told a colleague at the time, "I'm a lawyer. I know what *remand* means. It means a whole new hearing, new witnesses, a new trial. Yes! At least that's what it ought to be." Evans did not know then that the FPC "trial judge" was not only furious about this decision, he was irrevocably pro-dam, and determined to issue a new license come "hell or high water."

Evans talked the Sierra Club's leadership into taking a chance on letting him file for Intervention status. The odds were against it, but it was well worth the time and expense to take a shot.

"Remember," says Evans, "there was no such thing in 1967 as "environmental law." NEPA and the Clean Air Act were a full three years away; the Clean Water Act, five years out, and the Endangered Species Act not even a gleam in Senator Henry Jackson's eye. There was nothing out there; no guidance, no precedents, no law review articles. Nothing. Not even the *word* 'environment.'"

Evans fashioned an historic request to the Supreme Court. He recalls it saying something like, "Hey, you never heard of me before, but I just read this opinion, see, and I have a question: If the case has been remanded for a new trial, does that mean that any new parties can intervene?"

Evans enjoyed imagining the bemused contempt at such temerity from the provinces on the part of a court official when first reading the letter.

A month later he received a brief response, indicating he could intervene if he wanted to.

Armed with the letter, Evans paid a quick visit to the King County Courthouse in Seattle and requested a book covering the proper form of letters of appeal and petitions for legal intervention. Evans said they did not know what he was asking for and that was his first inkling that he might be plowing new ground.

It dawned on him that "there was no body of environmental law, cases or procedures – nothing, nada. This was to be, in lawyer language, a case entirely *de novo* (brand new)."

Back in his office, Evans began his due diligence by reading all the materials he could find about Hells Canyon and its values, along with literature about rivers. He dictated a petition for intervention with many "whereases" and reasons why the Sierra Club – which to his knowledge had never been involved in any sort of legal proceeding before – was qualified to present evidence about why Hells Canyon and the Snake River were more valuable to the public in a free-flowing state.

The next moment of inspiration was the recognition that there were two courts in which he was fighting and he had to win in both "the court of law" and the "court of public opinion."

Given the overwhelming pro-dam climate of the times in the Northwest, Evans was certain the Sierra Club and he personally were going to be attacked by pro-dam politicians and a sympathetic media. He knew the antidote must be demonstrating that they also had a solid and growing base of public support – local, regional and national.

For Evans this translated into a need to entice other plaintiffs and/or friends of the court. This was a daunting challenge. Evans knew he had much to do and little time

Brock Evans to the Rescue

Once a tree hugger, always a tree hugger; Evans hugs an old Bull Pine in the canyon. Photo: Brock Evans

to do it.

He tracked down the president of the Sierra Club, Edgar Wayburn, and the president of the Federation of Western Outdoor Clubs, Kenneth Baldwin. Together they headed up two national organizations that had influential local affiliates. After obtaining their permissions, Evans searched Idaho for a likely "local" candidate.

He found the co-plaintiff in the Idaho Alpine Club, a group already engaged in the fight at the local and state level. He had, inadvertently, stumbled onto some of the finest eco-warriors in Idaho. Jerry Jayne, Russ Brown, Boyd Norton, Pete Henault, and Jim Campbell agreed to sign on as a party to Evans' petition. A few months later, they reconstituted themselves and formed the organization that became the passionate heart and soul of the entire campaign thenceforth: the Hells Canyon Preservation Council itself.

The deadline ominously loomed, and Evans felt himself being pulled different directions. He likened the situation to being a piece of hamburger slid up and down a board, with each issue taking a bite out of the rapidly diminishing whole. These other issues were overwhelming his one-person operation.

The petition did get finished, with the required thirty duplicate copies painfully created. At 11:40 p.m. on the evening of August 31, 1967, Evans deposited them, duly stamped and dated, at the Post Office desk at Sea-Tac Airport for the next flight to Washington, and the headquarters of the Federal Power Commission.

As far as Evans knew, it was the first time anyone had ever tried to bring a legal action of any kind to rescue a "special place" in the Northwest.

Evans later confessed he really didn't know what he was doing. He set precedent after precedent that will always be a part of his legacy.

Curious about what would happen, Evans nonetheless was shaken by the vitriolic reaction. Interest groups working with and for the dambuilders were numerous and included companies like Boise's Morrison/Knudsen, which in early 1960s had won the contract to build the almost finished Teton Dam in eastern Idaho. Many other companies had home state senators in their pockets.

Some companies intimated others, especially outsiders, that they were close to and had a cozy thing going on with the "trial judge."

Here came this upstart Sierra Club and Idaho Alpine Club, filing a case saying the Snake River, as it flows through Hells Canyon, ought to be a *wild* river. For many of the vested interests, this was heresy which fostered genuine outrage. Corporate attorneys quivered in righteous indignation from Portland to Boise.

The first call Evans received was from the senior partner in the Seattle law firm he had left just a few months earlier. He later said he wasn't surprised since his old firm represented the Washington Public Power Supply

Brock Evans to the Rescue

System. They were representing the consortium of public power companies that were challenging the license already awarded to the private companies.

Evans said his old boss was polite as he queried him: just who and what was this Sierra Club, and what, really, did they want? Evans believed his former boss had received an angry call from Hugh Smith, lead attorney in Portland, for the privates. Smith had apparently gone to his copy of Martindale-Hubble, which lists all accredited attorneys in the country. There Smith found Evans' name, as still with his old firm.

Evans says he firmly and politely replied to his former boss that dams had already killed too many of the great rivers of the Northwest. He said the Sierra Club and its allies were going to convince the FPC that the license should be rejected. He further added the Sierra Club was going to argue that the Snake River should be a wild river in perpetuity.

Evans soon received a summons from the trial judge telling him to appear with all the other parties at a preliminary hearing at the Portland Federal Courthouse on September 27, 1967.

Evans recalls that his "heart sank." He had no idea what went on in such a hearing and fear of the unknown began to consume him.

Evans said it was about this time he realized he was more than just a lawyer working for the Sierra Club. He was the Northwest representative for the club and it was his job to represent the its policy stances and issues across one vast area, not just on Hells Canyon. The Glacier Peak Wilderness bill in Washington was about to be marked up in the Senate and was soon renamed the North Cascades National Park and Wilderness Area (See John McPhee's great essay in *Encounters with the Archdruid.*). It needed careful baby-sitting and lobbying. On Oregon's west side, Evans was trying to rally folks to make one last effort to save the magnificent forests of French Pete Creek chainsaws. In addition, the struggle over monster freeways in Seattle was at a fever pitch. Evans felt he needed help.

He called an old hiking and climbing friend, Tom Brucker, who was five years older, an experienced trial lawyer, a confident hard-to-rattle personality. A great conservationist at heart, Brucker liked the idea of trying to save a rare and precious place like Hells Canyon.

Before Evans could turn around, the hearing date was on them. The parties gathered at the Old Federal Courthouse in Portland. Thirty attorneys milled around in the ancient, oak-paneled courtroom waiting for the judge. Parties interested included contractors for private utilities and public agencies, smelling a fat cow. There were lawyers for subcontractors, consultants and specialized engineers.

Attorneys for various Indian nations, chambers of commerce, unions, upstream irrigators and power users in the region were present. These were the "players" who had divided up, then plugged, the Northwest's great rivers for the previous three decades. Twenty-eight of the thirty attorneys favored the dam. Evans said he felt intimidated and lonely.

He vividly recalls the scene: "We assembled in a semicircle under the judge's bench, Tom and I at the far end. The judge scowled down at us, saying, 'Each party will now make its opening statement.'

"I listened for clues about what we were up against, politically and as matters of law. After awhile, I realized my friend and I were receiving a daunting, yet fascinating insight into the psyches of those who held the power to destroy the Northwest's rivers, and had done so. Lawyer after lawyer recited his client's interests and its stake in the proposed dam in Hells Canyon, and why it had to be built. Some supported one builder, others another. Each delivered a compelling speech about why there had to be this one last dam.

Brock Evans to the Rescue

"It took all morning. Just before noon, the judge finally got to me. He leaned over the bench, scowled again, 'Mr. Evans, does the Sierra Club *really* have anything else to add to these proceedings?'"

"'Well, yes, Your Honor, if it please the Court,' I stammered, sure that my voice was squeaking some kind of falsetto. The Sierra Club believes that the highest and best use of the Snake River in Hells Canyon is in its free-flowing, natural state, and we intend to put on a case which will demonstrate this fact. We believe that there are other ways to provide the electric power the Northwest needs, but there is no way to replace what will be lost if the dam is built.'"

"I could almost *feel* the eyeballs rolling, hear the faint snorts of contempt, sense the head-shaking behind me, as the other lawyers audibly shifted in their seats. I thought I could hear their whispers: "This Sierra Club stuff is for real. He really means it. What idiocy!"

"But now, at last, the words had been said–in public. We were there. We would fight to the finish for the great gorges of the Snake. I felt a strange exhilaration as I walked back to my chair, a sensation which overrode my foreboding of the huge and mostly unknown task ahead of us. There would be no turning back now."

While every year in the 30-year fight to protect Hells Canyon was critical, 1968 had enough drama to last anyone a lifetime. On the national scene Americans were increasingly turning against involvement in the Vietnam war. Too many communities were seeing sons or daughters come home in body bags.

The presidential election turned topsy-turvy when incumbent President Lyndon Baines Johnson stunned the nation by renouncing his candidacy for re-election following a poor showing in the New Hampshire primary against the challenge from the cerebral Minnesota Senator Eugene McCarthy. With LBJ dropping out, the pressure for New York

Senator Robert Kennedy to pick up the fallen torch became too much for him to refuse. RFK's tragic assassination following his victory over McCarthy in the June 5 California primary virtually guaranteed a chaotic, dysfunctional Democratic convention that summer in Chicago.

When the smoke and tear gas cleared the Democratic nominee was the other long-time Minnesota senator, Hubert H. Humphery, then the sitting vice president. The "Happy Warrior" never stood a chance against former vice president Richard Nixon, who created a juggernaut that easily dispatched the Democratic nominee.

This change in administrations was to have some good consequences in the fight to protect the canyon, much to the surprise of the environmental community and the future members of the Hells Canyon Preservation Council.

There was another election in 1968 that also had consequences for Hells Canyon – the defeat of veteran Oregon Senator Wayne Morse by an almost unknown Republican state legislator, Bob Packwood. Over 100,000 ballots were challenged by one side or the other with Packwood finally being declared the winner by 3,500 votes.

Brock Evans would take full advantage of the opportunity to enlist this ambitious Packwood into his cause.

Evans knew his immediate challenge was to expand the base of support for protecting the canyon and set about proselytizing wherever he could get an audience. Early in the year, he was cheered by the news that he had a closet ally in the professional staff of the Federal Power Commission.

The staff told Evans to let them handle the wild rivers case, they knew how and had the resources and personnel to do it. Evans welcomed the assistance.

He recalled that one of his challenges was to convince sympathizers who had fought and lost other battles that they really could win this one. To enable more supporters to come forward, Evans took the unprecedented step of demanding two public hearings –

one scheduled for Lewiston, a pro-dam city, and another in Portland where there would be more supporters.

Evans felt the hearing in Lewiston was a draw, but that in Portland they smashed the pro-dam folks. HCPC folks did outstanding jobs in organizing, speaking, and publicity work. With those hearings, Evans felt public opinion was starting to turn their way.

Evans cross-examined witnesses by day, and appeared on Idaho Public TV exhorting the public at night. Power company attorneys tried to get him barred from the legal proceedings because he was "too political." He explained he was the only one available to the Sierra Club and had to do double duty. The judge agreed and he was readmitted.

Evans and others reaffirmed the notion they should seek comprehensive legislation to protect the entire canyon, not just the river. They knew they needed a champion in Congress and were not sure who that would be.

At the end of the year, they received disheartening news: Interior Secretary Stewart Udall came out in support of the Appaloosa site for a federally built dam which was what Idaho Senator Jordan had favored before adopting Idaho Power's' three smaller dams approach. The Johnson Administration was a lame duck though, and Evans resolved, contrary as it seems, to take a run at the new Nixon Administration come January, 1969.

In the late winter of 1969, Evans headed to Washington, D.C., to make his case. Calling in favors and capitalizing on his ability to find and nurture good relationships, Evans felt his goal of getting the Nixon administration to reverse Udall's pro-federal dam position was obtainable. He also figured he could arrange a meeting with key Nixon aide John Erlichmann, who Evans knew somewhat as a fellow attorney from his days practicing law in Seattle.

Evans said the meeting went well. He quoted Erlichman as saying "I am a fanatic environmentalist, Brock," Erlichman also arranged a meeting between Evans and new Interior Undersecretary, Russell Train. Shortly thereafter, Train announced Interior opposition to any dam.

Later in that winter, newly elected Oregon Senator Bob Packwood let Evans, the Sierra Club and the Hells Canyon Preservation Counsel know he would like to help the Hells Canyon legislation, up to and including, sponsorship of a bill.

Evans made a rare mistake: He accepted Packwood's offer and proceeded to meet with the senator's staff. He failed to touch base with Idaho's two senators, Frank Church and Len B. Jordan, who were starting to put distance between them and Packwood. They saw Packwood as an overly ambitious senator with little respect for his elders.

Packwood appeared to be seeking full credit for whatever compromise was worked out and showed no patience for the seven and a half year moratorium on dam building or the study of dam construction in Hells Canyon until the preferred approach was worked out. Church and Jordan were senators held in high regard by colleagues and much deference was afforded them. In the fall, their bill passed, while Packwood was given a lesson in humility; his bill languished in committee, partly to put the upstart freshman in his place.

Moratorium notwithstanding, the next seven years were far from quiet. Church, in particular, put staff to work preparing legislation that could be addressed by both sides. Looking back to his own tough re-election fight in 1968, Church recognized the shifting of the democratic north towards a Republican forecast was potential trouble.

FRANK CHURCH, LBJ & THE POLITICS OF HELL

IN THE INTRODUCTION to the section of Frank Church's papers dealing with Hells Canyon, his long-time legal counsel, Fred Hutchison, wrote:

"One of the earliest speeches Frank Church delivered on the Senate floor (March 7, 1957) was in support of the construction of the Hells Canyon Dam in Idaho. Church stated that 'water is the life-blood of our economy in Idaho.' The speech summarized his support of the building of the dam for the "development of our great rivers – a tradition that has served the people well and contributed much to the building of west."

The papers in the series reflect Senator Church's evolving view on dam construction in Hells Canyon region.

The question is raised continuously in this series as to the types of dams to be built, the size, the costs, and who should build, control, and benefit from them. During the 1960s opposition to the construction of dams increased based on environmental concerns. As the country entered the 1970s, the perception of Hells Canyon began to include environmental considerations. A moratorium on dam building was proposed by Secretary of the Interior Walter J. Hickel in 1969 to restrict the uses of the Snake River. Senators Church and Jordan introduced legislation in 1970 supporting a 10-year moratorium to evaluate the needs of users.

In 1973, Frank Church proposed permanent protection for the Middle Snake River and the Hells Canyon area, stating the people can no longer look at any region with tunnel vision. A bill was written to create a

Hells Canyon wilderness area on the undeveloped portion of the Middle Snake and to protect upstream water rights and grazing.

Church's evolving views reflected not just an awareness of a growing environmental ethos in America, but also a belief that Idahoans of all persuasions were more willing than ever before to take stands supporting environmental protection.

Church also had to have taken heart from his November 1968 victory over one of the best one-on-one campaigners in Idaho history, Second District Republican Congressman George Hansen. Church defeated the hard right Hansen by what turned out to be his largest victory margin in any of his four Senate races: taking 60% of the vote.

Another reason the debate over whether to dam became a national issue had nothing to do with Floyd Harvey or Brock Evans or the emerging leaders of the still-in-the-future Hells Canyon Preservation Council. It had everything to do with the then U.S. Senate's Democratic Majority Leader, Texas Senator Lyndon Baines Johnson, and his presidential ambitions.

LBJ will always remain somewhat of an anomaly in American politics.

The normal rules of the political game do not reward the inveterate liar and LBJ clearly was that. Yet, he made it to the top and his masterful handling of the potential dams in Hells Canyon as trade bait to help secure fairly modest changes to America's civil rights laws is a superb example of his leadership skills.

Besides being a great tactician, LBJ was an excellent "psycho-analyst" of what made each of his congressional colleagues tick. He studied them all carefully, developing a sense of their strengths and weaknesses. He had an insidious and insightful formula: "Tell me a man's mother's ambitions for him and his father's failures and I can take the measure of the man."

Robert Caro tells the story in volume three of his incomparable five-volume biography of Lyndon Johnson, entitled *Master of the Senate.* Unfortunately, the fact-checker Caro was using did not catch some errors, the net effect of which serves to raise a few doubts about the basic story itself. Nonetheless the story warrants reciting when laying out the political history of Hells Canyon and its history.

As a Southerner, Johnson knew that to achieve his life-long goal of becoming president he had to address the festering issue of race relations. Well aware of "Jim Crow" laws throughout the South that discriminated against African-Americans; Johnson had to "redo" his image.

In his younger years as a member of Congress, Johnson could "race bait" with the best. In order to rise to majority leader relatively soon after arriving at the Senate, Johnson carefully cultivated the old bulls of the Senate, the southern Democrats who by seniority held powerful committee chairmanships.

Without alienating these crucial colleagues, he also had to placate liberal northern Democratic senators, such as Minnesota's Hubert Humphrey. Looking down the road towards the 1960 presidential election, Johnson decided that the modest changes made to the basic Civil Rights Act was just the ticket.

Johnson soon learned in negotiations with the bloc of twenty-two southern Democrat's that they would only accept small changes in the voting laws and it had to have a jury trial amendment. Anything more would prompt a filibuster and it required two-thirds of the Senate to break the hold up.

LBJ succeeded in walking the tightrope. When he needed to show the good 'ol boys of the South he could defeat almost any amendment, he would flash the votes he had in his back pocket – liberal, western senators who had bought into his *quid pro quo*, the federally built High Hells Canyon Dam, in exchange for votes that would limit interference in state elections and jury trials for race-related matters.

With 20/20 hindsight, historians today marvel at the normally pro-civil rights senators who bought LBJ's "joy juice." The roll call of those hornswoggled by LBJ includes Senators Henry Jackson and Warren Magnuson of Washington; Frank Church of Idaho; Mike Mansfield of Montana; and, the iconic Wayne Morse of Oregon.

There were multiple ironies in the eventual outcome. LBJ obtained his Civil Rights legislation without having to use the votes of the liberal western senators, which, of course, kept his options open as he wheeled and dealed toward a presidential nomination to which he felt entitled.

He also gauged the House correctly. There were not enough votes to launch the High Hells Canyon Dam construction. That too left him with options. LBJ was a legendary wheeler and dealer, but few believe he ever would have become president had he not been John Kennedy's vice president when the latter was assassinated in 1963.

Neither is there much question that the "shadow deal" angered the tried and true liberal senators who supported tougher civil rights legislation.

Illinois Senator Paul Douglas termed the possible deal "counterfeit money." He felt it was another example of LBJ's profound cynicism, that some of his western colleagues had been thoroughly bamboozled. Had the deal been done, it would have only given the western apostates the ability to claim victory, not victory itself. That would have required the full support of Johnson's Texas colleague, Speaker Sam Rayburn. Despite Rayburn's fondness for Johnson, he wasn't about to buck the majority of the House over some Idaho dam project.

Caro tells a wonderful anecdote at the end of the flawed chapter on Hells Canyon. When campaigning for the presidency early in 1960, LBJ stopped in Idaho Falls. The local Democrats had organized a decent turn out for the brief event and Senator Church was leading the delegation of folks lined up along the fence which LBJ, was working.

When he came to Church, he looked him in the eye and asked if his presence at the rally constituted an endorsement of his candidacy. Church stuttered that he hadn't made up his mind.

Johnson, though, had read Church's eyes. On the way back to his plane, LBJ turned to George Reedy, his press secretary, and said, "That son of a bitch Church is going to go for Kennedy." He then speculated that the Kennedy people had offered Church more than he could, the "keynoter" slot at the Democratic convention. LBJ took it personally and never forgave Church.

After all, when Church first came to the Senate, LBJ had taken him under wing and later had given him a coveted slot on the Foreign Relations Committee over senators with more seniority.

Fortunately, LBJ never carried out anything punitive against any of the three. Neither did he forget.

There are some major flaws in Caro's chapter on Hells Canyon related to geography and history. Caro, for whatever reason, incorrectly placed Hells Canyon in the middle of the Sawtooths. He also claims the Republican governors of Oregon and Idaho lost their re-election bids because of their support for Idaho Power to be the entity to build any dams in Hells Canyon.

Not so. Oregon Republican Governor Elmo Smith lost in 1956 to the Democratic candidate, Robert Holmes. There was no gubernatorial race in Idaho in 1956. In 1954, Len Jordan, who did support Idaho Power, completed the one term he was allowed to serve because of a one-term limit law. His successor, Republican Attorney General Robert Smylie, was able to get the law reversed during his first term. He was re-elected in 1958 and in 1962. Seeking a fourth term in 1966, Smylie was defeated in the Republican primary by Sandpoint state senator Don Samuelson.

In 1956, former Oregon Governor Doug "Give-away" McKay, who was serving as President Dwight D. Eisenhower's Secretary of the Interior, came back to Oregon to run against incumbent Wayne Morse. Oregon's senior senator wanted public power to build any dam in Hells Canyon. McKay saw himself as the defender of free enterprise and was strongly supported by private power interests throughout the Northwest.

McKay proved to be no match for Morse, who won easily.

In Idaho, the issue of public vs. private power building dams in Hells Canyon carried through several election cycles, starting in 1948.

In the 1956 Democratic primary, Idaho Power opposed both of the leading Democratic contenders, former Senator Glen Taylor, and young Boise attorney Frank Church. Taylor and Church were strong advocates of public power. Church won the primary by a scant and controversial 200 votes and went on to win in the general election.

The new senator had the beginnings of a solid background on the issues surrounding the Hells Canyon debate, knowledge which he put to good use as other events unfolded.

The Idaho Statesman, which rarely endorsed a Democrat, so detested Welker that in the general election they went with Church.

As Church aide Hutchison points out, two of the first remarks made by Church on arriving at the Senate in 1957 were on the subject of Hells Canyon. In fact, when South Dakota Senator George McGovern sent a letter to senatorial colleagues asking what they thought was their best speech ever, Church offered his maiden speech on the floor of the Senate on May 15, 1957 which was about the case for a high federal dam in the canyon.

The Idaho senator's first remarks in any D.C. forum came on March 7, 1957, before the Interior Committee's subcommittee on Irrigation and Reclamation. In a move that had to be well-liked by the Committee of Nine, Church cast the issue of the high federal dam in the light of preserving and protecting up-stream water rights.

Church believed that Idaho's economic future was dependent on the high dam being built. He said the Snake River belonged to the people of Idaho, that the site of the proposed high dam called for a dam to match its great dimensions. He claimed Congress had a duty not to let the site be wasted.

He refuted arguments put forth by Idaho Power and the private consortium supporting a privately constructed and dam.

Church brilliantly termed Idaho's economy a "colonial economy" and pointed out that private utilities were claiming the net result of their building dams would be power at a reasonable 6.69 mills per/kilowatt hour (kwh). Church argued that federal construction would result in electricity being sold for 2.65 mills per/kwh. It was a powerful piece of testimony, the likes of which were seldom heard in the hallowed halls of Congress.

On May 15, 1957, Church rose on the Senate floor to seek support for Senate Bill 555, that would authorize construction of a high dam by the federal government. It was his maiden speech and judging from the compliments and platitudes colleagues tossed his way, it was an outstanding performance.

Church began with a candid admission that his was

Idaho Senator Frank Church. Photo: BSU archives

in all probability opposed by a majority of his constituents. "I must concede at the outset, that the long, determined and resourceful indoctrination campaign against a high government dam in Hells Canyon (by Idaho Power) has proved highly effective in Idaho."

Church said mail and phone calls to his office were 2 to 1 against his view.

He refuted Idaho Power's arguments, adding a new dimension, one that proved difficult for Idaho Power to counter. He debunked the argument that it would cost the taxpayer less to have private enterprise build the dam than the federal government. He simply pointed out that the cost of borrowing the money to build the project by the private consortium would be 4.5%, whereas the borrowing cost for the federal government would be 2.5%.

He finished by underscoring that his predecessor, the revered Senator William Borah, Idaho's lion in the Senate, had on several occasions made it clear he thought there was plenty of room for public and private power in the region.

During the next ten years, Church monitored the progress towards excluding dams and ultimately protecting the canyon. In 1962, Len Jordan was appointed to the other senate seat and then won the seat in a special election. It is fair to say that the two bonded and respected the other. Jordan, because he had lived in the canyon and was an expert on Idaho water law, received increasing deference from Church. By 1968, they were drawn back into the fray by the efforts of the junior senator from Oregon, Bob Packwood, to seize the lead on protecting the canyon by introducing a bill largely written by Brock Evans, as mentioned earlier.

When Jordan retired from the Senate, Jim McClure took the seat. Church's natural resources advisor Mike Wetherall worked on several drafts of a moratorium bill that would be acceptable to McClure, Governor Andrus of Idaho, Governor McCall of Oregon and Oregon senators, Packwood and Mark Hatfield.

On July 23, 1973, Church introduced the Hells Canyon National Recreation Area legislation. It would become the vehicle for negotiations between the House and Senate. On June 4 a compromise measure passed the Senate and was signed into law as Public Law 94-199 on December 31, 1975.

On June 20, 1976 members of the Idaho and Oregon congressional and state delegations took part in the formal dedication of the Hells Canyon NRA. In his moving remarks on the occasion, Church went out of his way to single out and praise McClure for his critical and constructive role.

JUST AROUND THE BEND

LOOKING BACK ON IT NOW through the mist of the years, it seems to Brock Evans the entire saga of the canyon was more like an Icelandic epic than anything else. Certainly, it was a tale of David and Goliath: great odds faced and somehow overcome, a huge and most unlikely victory snatched from the jaws of defeat.

Evans was particularly eloquent on this point. He wrote in an essay "real epics, are <u>not</u> about the deeds of gods and goddesses who just fly around and do magic as a matter of course. Epics are what <u>ordinary</u> people do, rising to scary and demanding occasions and stumbling through them no matter what." (See Rick Johnson's foreword).

Evans often suffered from a "needless anxiety complex," constantly worrying about how well he was performing his duties, and whether his love for the canyon had caused him to relegate equally important issues to the back burner. He was overwhelmed by the magnitude of the task which lay ahead – how to rescue Hells Canyon – and grappling with other issues popping up across the Northwest.

For solace he would sometimes call to mind his hiring by one of the giant leaders of the environmental movement, David Brower, in early-1967. Just to be around a living legend was impressive. It was Brower who let him know the extent of his territory: "When I first came on the scene, it was from Brower that I learned my 'territory' was, literally, everything from the North Pole to San Francisco, and as far east as Yellowstone. Northwest North America, from Alaska to the North Cascades to the

Oregon Cascades, from the Sawtooths to the Flathead to the Wind River, and every place in between. I was the only full-time paid person north of San Francisco and I felt responsible for the fate of Hells Canyon – at least accountable for putting together a campaign that we all could rally around and have a chance of success."

Evans says that since he hadn't yet met anyone from the just-formed HCPC, except for a small and courageous nucleus of local folks, he felt quite alone.

Evans had another more personal concern: He had literally as well as figuratively fallen in love with Hells Canyon. From the first time he had journeyed through Hells Canyon, he was enchanted by its majesty and beauty. For him it was "as if some old lost chord had been plucked inside. My heart sang to a new kind of music I hadn't even known was there. I loved Hells Canyon, and vowed to give everything in my power to try to save it."

The campaign began with the Petition of Intervention Evans filed in August 1968 before the Federal Power Commission (FPC) challenging the issuance of the license to build the dam. Instead that the great river should be allowed to forever run free, the petition argued.

The Sierra Club and its "friends" at least were in the case, much to the ill-disguised disgust of dambuilders and hangers-on who had dominated Northwest river politics for decades. Evans knew, though, he had to prove they belonged.

"We have to do well in the case, if we hope even to just to slow down the dam juggernaut," he said at the time.

The odds appeared to be daunting because most observers knew that the trial judge would eventually issue another dam license to one of the contending parties. They had to do well, and they did by raising in a hostile forum an issue (wild river) never flagged before. It was all part of a sophisticated game plan Evans worked up.

The small band of Evans' insurgents, including HCPC leaders, met that fall. They worked out a two-part strategy: the FPC case immediately and the political follow up as they gained support.

The FPC case was vital to their goal because it would give them time to show the world the stunning canyon was worth saving and that the cause was not hopeless.

They knew they had to continue to do much in a short period of time. The better known legal tools of National Environmental Policy Act (NEPA) and Endangered Species Act (ESA) employed by environmentalists today were then years in the future. Evans continued to believe, and quietly to draft, a new law that would permanently save the great river, as well as its magnificent setting.

The odds were against the supreme political effort required to do this and it seemed more intimidating than the legal case. Northwest politics and politicians were still dominated by the "rivers want to work" philosophy, Incomprehensible as that may seem today, dams were the accepted wisdom.

Any notion of leaving a river "wild," un-dammed and free was heresy.

Furthermore, hostility to anything "preservationist" in conservative eastern Oregon and northern Idaho was visceral, and politically dangerous. Only a few brave locals, people like Ken Witty and John Barker, dared to buck conventional wisdom.

Oregon Senators Hatfield and Morse and Idaho's Jordan were firm dam supporters. Idaho's Church, a conservation hero, vacillated and was cautious with a re-election coming up. The political establishments of both states lined up in favor of the dams, and opposed to the upstarts who dared to challenge the existing order.

Evans knew a strong case for leaving a river wild

and free would thoroughly discombobulate the big dam adherents, and it did. It also created the opportunity to go national by piggy-backing on the better known Grand Canyon debate.

Evans proselytized reporters and friends, selling the notion that dams in Hells Canyon were every bit as obscene as dams in the Grand Canyon. The full page ads that the Sierra Club ran in the *Washington Post* and the *New York Times* depicting a flooded Sistine Chapel and then asking people if they wanted to flood one of the more beautiful sights in the world akin to a natural Sistine Chapel hit a chord with millions of people who were galvanized to contribute money and write letters to their congressional delegations.

Evans and co-counsel Tom Brucker began to search for credible advocates for a wild river. This was no small endeavor because this was a time period in the West in which most towns tried to present unified faces on the tough issues of the day.

Although they located good witnesses to speak about the river's wildlife and its stunning geology, and persuaded famed scientist Luna Leopold to contribute a seminal work quantifying the economic and social values of a wild river, Evans felt more was needed.

Evans knew, too, the Sierra Club and his co-petitioners had to be credible about the "electric power" issue, since it had dared to challenge the conventional wisdom.

They had to answer these claims with something tangible and effective. Conservation, in itself, was not deemed consequential then. Only one other possibility presented itself: nuclear power. In those innocent times, it seemed a good option. Nearly all the early movers and shakers within HCPC itself were Idahoans employed by the INL facility west of Idaho Falls, so there was strong support.

The Sierra Club advocated for nuclear power in a court of law. It came to pass in 1968.

That was the strategic and human context of the high-stress, exhilarating times of the late 60s. Not many people thought the anti-dam effort could win. So Evans spent the 1968 summer traveling throughout Idaho and eastern Oregon, organizing strong turnouts at public hearings that were to be held.

In Lewiston especially, the "home turf" of the dambuilders, Evans put considerable effort into persuading an older group of weary, too-often-defeated environmentalists to testify. Getting them to believe again was a critical piece of Evans' strategy.

At the hearing, Evans felt the Sierra Club and its allies held the opposition to a draw. In Portland, however, he rated it a substantial victory. He gave the lion's share of the credit for success at both hearings to HCPC folks, led by John Barker, Russ Brown, Floyd Harvey, Pete Henault, Jerry Jayne, Russ Mager, Jack Barry, and Al McGlinsky. Carmelita Holland and Steve Moenrin from Oregon also performed above and beyond, working well with Idahoans who also attended the Portland hearing, displaying great skill at organizing, speaking, and publicity.

Evans says 1969 was just a blur of coalition building, in Washington, D.C. and the Pacific Northwest, but he was encouraged. He said he could feel sentiment growing on a national scale for protecting Hells Canyon along with the Grand Canyon. Unfortunately, the Glens Canyon Dam moved ahead.

Many years back, when the kids and I were returning from a hike in central Idaho, during a gas stop in Missoula, I grabbed the local paper, The Missoulian. The paper contained a story called "The Ten Most Common Lies told on the Trail." It was a list of the fibs every parent for generations has told young children when on a hike to encourage them to keep walking and not collapse in a trail of tears.

I was ten for ten. I had employed every one of the fibs. The classic was saying that the end of the trail was "just around the next bend." During the early 70s Brock Evans must have several times felt that victory in the form of a protective bill was just ahead, just around the next bend. It wasn't so – there was five years to go.

In 1970, Evans took full advantage of the second Earth Day in April and tied the publicity generating across the country to Earth Day, a celebration of saving as much of the natural beauty left in America. Hells Canyon had to be at the top of lists.

In May, Evans and some of the HCPC leadership scored a national media coup when they convinced an NBC News film crew to tag along with them as they accompanied Oregon Senator Packwood on a float trip through the canyon. When NBC's television special ran later in the year, it provoked a national outcry of opposition to a dam in Hells Canyon.

Following this excursion, the junior senator from Oregon introduced his own bill that had largely been worked up by the staff, Evans, the Sierra Club and the Hells Canyon Preservation Council. It reflected premature discussions Evans had had with the senator and key staff while the group camped their first night on the river near Granite Creek.

Evans said the draft had boundaries, acreage and land uses that would be determined according to criteria worked out at Granite Creek. Unfortunately for Packwood, neither of Idaho's two senators, Frank Church and Len Jordan, signed on as co-sponsors.

In part deciding to put the ambitious but junior Packwood in his place, Church and Jordan introduced the now seven-year moratorium on studies on dams of any kind in the canyon and furthermore forbade any studies that might advocate interbasin transfer of water.

In late fall, Len B. Jordan made headlines in the D.C.- area media. He was about to leave his apartment building to walk the few blocks to the Capitol to attend the annual National Prayer Breakfast. On entering the apartment building's elevator he noted the presence of a young man. As soon as the elevator door closed, the stranger intimated he had a gun in his pocket and demanded the 70-year-old senator hand over his billfold.

Before the would-be-robber could react, Jordan hauled off with a haymaker that stunned the assailant, who managed to hit the senator on his forehead in retaliation. By then the elevator had reached the main floor, the doors opened and the senator's assailant fled. Jordan continued on his way to the prayer breakfast with a noticeable lump on his forehead.

He said not a word to anyone, nor did he make a report with law enforcement, figuring it would do little good.

Late in the day, he casually mentioned the incident to his executive secretary, Gwen Lewis. She knew a good press story when she heard it and had Jordan's press secretary, Gary Catron, leak the story to Dick Charnock in the Boise office of UPI. Charnock filed a story that the D.C. media immediately picked up and published.

Needless to say the senator was the toast of the town for a few days. Back home in Idaho it further served to burnish the senator's solid reputation and considerably dampened speculation in some quarters that Jordan was getting too old and too tired and should not run again.

The two years of 1971 and 1972 were the most critical years in the epic saga of efforts to prevent dams and protect the beauty of Hells Canyon.

As mentioned, Senator Packwood had introduced his protection bill for the canyon, but he filed it as a substitute measure replace of the Church/Jordan seven-year moratorium measure.

Jordan fired back immediately, charging that Packwood's bill was vague, premature, lacked the necessary supportive data. It was deliberately designed to be nothing less than an emotional appeal to national conservation groups to flood members of Congress with supportive pleas to protect the canyon.

In an interview with the A. Robert Smith News Bureau (which covered the D.C. scene for a number of western and Alaskan newspapers), Jordan served notice to Packwood that the bill's language with regard to prioritizing upstream water rights was significantly deficient. He also slammed the Oregon senator for trying to rush his bill through Congress before the Forest Service had completed studies on land-use patterns in the canyon.

Given the rocky relationship between Packwood and his Pacific Northwest colleagues, it was unlikely his bill would receive a hearing before the committee on the Interior and Insular Affairs.

In early July, following the Federal Power Commission's hearing examiner weighing in for a dam at the Low Mountain Sheep Pleasant Valley site, and the passage in late June by the Senate unanimously endorsing the Church-Jordan Moratorium bill, Oregon's second distict congressman, Al Ullman, the soon-to-be-chair of the powerful House Ways and Means committee, weigh-in on the issue.

Ullman, guessing that Packwood's bill would still get a hearing in the fall despite its rejection as a substitute for the Church-Jordan moratorium, served notice that he would not be adverse to a five-year moratorium on any dam planning or building on the Middle Snake in Hells Canyon. His statement to the media, however, was wrapped around language expressing concern about a looming energy crisis brought on by shortages in major power production.

Ullman underscored that he was absolutely opposed to Packwood's bill making the middle Snake a protected national river. He hinted strongly that following the five-year moratorium he might well support construction of a dam because he felt America was on the verge of a power crisis.

    The Oregon congressman also took shots at Church and at Jordan, saying he did not understand why Church had such a sense of urgency about having a moratorium and that the latter did not care about the looming energy crisis.

    While Church was a bit surprised by Ullman's truculence, he was stunned by the blind-side attack on his support for a moratorium from Boyd Norton, a leading environmentalist. Norton blasted Church in a critical article he wrote for *Not Man Apart*, the monthly newspaper for the Friends of the Earth.

    Norton had lived in Idaho, but moved to Colorado to become a field director for the Friends. Norton's language was hyperbolic and insulting. He labeled the Church/Jordan moratorium a "sellout to the reclamation dam builders" and that Church was vindictively fighting Packwood and his Snake National River bill.

    Church decided to take the high road. Asked to comment after being shown the article, the senior Idaho senator declined to respond, saying he did not want to get into a fight with people that shared the same goals. "We're both seeking the same objective. We just disagree on the tactics."

    Nevertheless, he was clearly angry and deeply disappointed that Norton questioned his integrity. For the senator, it was an unwarranted attack and from that time forward he wrote Norton off.

    One could also tell that more than ever the Idaho senator was looking forward to the upcoming hearing on the Packwood bill.

The fact that Packwood was even getting a hearing before Nevada Senator Alan Bible's subcommittee on Parks and Recreation was due in no small part to Church, Jordan and Hatfield asking Bible to approve a hearing. Packwood was provided the rope to hang himself.

The date was September 16th, 1971, and the tranquility was about to go the way of the buffalo. It became clear Packwood was playing to the environmental protection interests concerned about how Hells Canyon was going to be protected, not to those Oregonians living adjacent to the canyon.

It is a safe assumption that even Brock Evans and Pete Henault, two of Packwood's most ardent supporters, had no idea that Packwood envisioned this issue as a possible launch of a bid to be president. There can be no other explanation for someone as bright as Packwood to fatally wound his own bill. Kill it he did, however.

At the outset of the hearing, Church, echoing the concerns raised earlier by Jordan, made it obvious he shared the goal of Packwood's bill, i.e., protection of the free-flowing waters of the middle Snake.

Church bent over backwards trying to show Packwood that all his flawed bill needed for passage was stronger language clarifying the priority of water rights and the bedrock principle of first in time, first in right.

The Oregon senator refused to budge.

At the end of the first day's hearing one senator's aide was heard saying to a friend, "A guy can either play to the audience or play to the committee. Packwood is playing to the audience." His bill never made it out of the subcommittee.

Evans chose to make lemonade out of the lemon, expressing his pleasure with Church and officially expressed his opposition to any dams in Hells Canyon. Despite strong sentiment for a dam, Evans saw the hearing as just another opportunity to explain to the public the rationale for protecting the river and the canyon. Incrementally, he felt their cause was making headway in its goal to crash through the news media wall that thus far had treated the matter as primarily one of regional interest only.

Two other matters at this time did much to shape the parameters of the issue in 1972. First, the Church/Jordan moratorium bill was unanimously adopted by the Senate which killed the Packwood Snake River bill as a substitute measure.

Oregon Senator Bob Packwood. Photo: Boise State University archives

Years later, in an interview, Evans confessed he never quite knew where and why the moratorium idea originated. He understood though the impact it had in stopping the momentum for a Hells Canyon National Park. He surmised it had much to do with the byzantine nature of Idaho politics, which he conceded were difficult, at best, for any non-Idahoan to understand.

Secondly, Jordan announced his intention not to seek another term in the Senate.

The announcement came as a surprise since just about every political pundit in the Northwest had concluded he was running and was a shoo-in for re-election. His decision set off a scramble in both parties for a successor. The future of Hells Canyon would, for certain, become an issue in the campaign.

In late 1971 the trial judge for the Federal Power Commission ended the hearings on whether to grant a license for a dam in Hells Canyon. In early 1972, he issued his opinion, and not surprisingly, he granted a dam license to the now-unified applicants. Surprisingly, though, he said the license would not take effect until the end of 1975.

Evans was pleased with this aspect because it allowed him three years grace to get his bill through Congress.

Also, as the calendar turned to 1972, Church acknowledged he expected to continue to see pressure from friends in the environmental community to abandon support for the Church/Jordan moratorium and instead toss his support to the Packwood bill.

Some thought that with Jordan having announced he was leaving the Senate, Church might choose to drop his alliance with Jordan. Those who thought this did not know Frank Church. He had given his word to Jordan and he would honor it.

Church hinted in media interviews he might introduce his own bill on the subject down the road, but at that time it would be premature. Church said he still wanted to see certain Forest Studies completed, and he also made it clear, particularly on the upcoming legislation to create a Sawtooth National Recreation Area (NRA), he would need Jordan's support.

Church further indicated he thought Representative Jim McClure, the GOP favorite to succeed Len Jordan, was going to become more and more of a player. His instincts were dead on.

It is fair to say McClure always had a mixed attitude towards the issue of dams in Hells Canyon. Initially, he was supportive, but while still a member of the House, he sent out a "self-selected" mail back survey, and was stunned to see that a solid majority of his constituency supported protecting the canyon and the river. Furthermore, they had no trust in the federal government to do the job.

Much to the surprise of his environmental critics, Jim McClure loved the Hells Canyon area, especially the hikes into the lakes scattered in the Seven Devils Mountains. McClure enjoyed backpacking and always took a fishing rod.

In mid-June 1972, less than two months before the primary to determine the Republican and Democratic nominees for Jordan's seat, McClure could not offer any assurances that the companion bill on a moratorium would be put before the House by Rep. Orval Hansen of Idaho and him or that it would gain passage.

McClure candidly acknowledged his support for a moratorium would undoubtedly benefit his Senate candidacy. He had a slightly different wrinkle, though. He felt another study by the USFS was in order before folks started taking immovable positions. Like Church and Jordan, McClure also had concerns about language referring to water rights.

Later that year, Rep. Ullman of Oregon, introduced his own legislation which tried to protect the forests of the Lower Minam River in eastern Oregon. Because Ullman was sponsoring the bill, it passed. Ullman was a critical component in Evans' game plan. Given this role, Evans was pleased with the support.

For Evans, this became a source of comfort. Others in eastern Oregon were motivated to speak out, joining ranks with the brave early ones like Ken Witty, Carmelita Holland, Loren Hughes, and Forest Service employees like Wade Hall.

In 1973, Ullman introduced another version of his National Recreation Area bill which forbid dams on the Snake, but it was weaker in protections for the wilderness

Scenic vista along Snake River trail. Photo: Marcia Carlson

on the plateau and allowed a road along the canyon rim.

The year 1973 also saw a changing of the guard in the Northwest's Sierra Club structure. Evans was promoted to head the Sierra Club office in Washington, D.C. Once there, he began to focus on the Alaska lands issue, but he stayed strongly committed to Hells Canyon and worked closely with Doug Scott, his successor as the Northwest field director. Scott took up the daily lobbying tasks, and did an effective job building further support.

In 1974, hearings were held on the Ullman bill, which was still controversial in Ullman's district. Supporters for protecting the canyon did well in eastern Oregon, and again overwhelmed opponents in the Portland hearing, thanks to organizing by HCPC and its President Pete Henault. Scott and Evans singled out the late Idaho Governor Cecil Andrus' support as influential.

Despite their praise, both later supported Hawaii Congresswoman Patsy Mink to be Jimmy Carter's

Secretary of the Interior. Fortunately, Carter ignored their recommendation and picked Andrus instead.

To this day, Evans bemoans that decision and readily concedes Andrus was the better selection and the right person at the right time in the right place, and especially the strategy for getting the Alaska lands properly protected.

Andrus said he had forgiven Evans and Scott, but he never forgot it, either.

In December 1974, a bill creating a Hells Canyon National Recreation Area was poised for passage, but Congressman Teno Roncalio, a Democrat from Reno, a strong dam proponent, seeing that Evans and Scott had the votes in the House Interior Committee to pass the Ullman bill, walked out, creating the lack of a quorum. The bill failed for that session of Congress.

The following year a final bill was passed and signed into law by President Gerald Ford on November 16, 1975. The Snake River was declared a Wild and Scenic River, the Asotin Dam was deauthorized, wilderness areas were created in the Seven Devils and Inner Canyon, while the Imnaha River and other tributaries were included in the 700,000 acre Hells Canyon National Recreation Area.

It seemed like victory at the time. In reality for the environmental community, the battle was only half won. In a classic case of "pigs get fat, but hogs get slaughtered," some of the environmental purists, especially those who still yearned for a national park status for the canyon, over-reached with a campaign to ban motorized craft (i.e. jet boats) on the river.

THE HELLS CANYON NRA ACT OF 1975

IN THE 1950s AND 60s there was little doubt in anyone's mind that a dam would be built somewhere on the Snake River in Hells Canyon. The only question was which dam or combination of dams would be built and who would build them, private or public power. Those entities took their fight to the Supreme Court where Justice William O. Douglas released the decision on June 5, 1967, a ruling that sent both parties back to the drawing boards.

This decision brought new life to the movement to protect the canyon from dam construction, the so-called "cement mixer boys." It culminated in passage of the Hells Canyon National Recreation Area Act in 1975, including the protective designation of 67.5 miles of the Snake River as wild or scenic.

Many people and organizations were important to passage of the Act, but no one was more so than Floyd Harvey, a power boat outfitter from Lewiston. Harvey mobilized support among local and regional environmental organizations. He played a key role in forming the Hells Canyon Preservation Council. He also elevated Hells Canyon's issues to national attention by jet boating celebrities into the canyon and enlisting their support. These included radio personality Arthur Godfrey and folk singer Burl Ives.

This law (PL94-199, November 16, 1975) designated 652,000 acres in Oregon and Idaho as the Hells Canyon National Recreation Area. Within the recreation area, it placed 214,000 acres of wilderness and 171 miles of rivers under wild and scenic designation. These include additions from the Oregon Wilderness and Omnibus

Rivers Acts, both of which postdate the HCNRA Act. The Snake River is designated wild from Hells Canyon Dam north to Pittsburg Landing (31.5 miles), scenic from Pittsburg Landing north to the Wallowa-Whitman National Forest's north boundary (36 miles) and study from the Wallowa-Whitman's north boundary to the HCNRA's north boundary and the Oregon / Washington state line (4 miles).

The National Park Service completed its study in 1980 and recommended designation of the "study" portion of the river as "scenic" from the present scenic boundary to Heller Bar and "recreation" from Heller Bar to the upper end of Lower Granite Reservoir at Asotin.

The study was held in the Department of the Interior until 1983 when it finally was released to the President with a cover memo saying that designation was not recommended at that time. When no legislation to designate the study river was introduced by 1986, the study protection expired and three organizations immediately filed to build the Asotin Dam. The resulting outrage was so widespread that Senators Steve Symms and James McClure introduced legislation which prohibited further dams on either the Middle Snake or Lower Salmon Rivers. It quickly became law.

None of the wild or scenic Snake River is within wilderness, although the half-mile wide corridor is bordered on both sides by wilderness for 18 miles and on one side for an additional 32 miles.

Some important sections of the act are:
- Section 7 which establishes management objectives;
- Section 8 which requires a comprehensive management plan (CMP);
- Section 10, which addresses the promulgation of regulations and recognize both motorized and non-motorized craft as valid uses of the Snake River.

Regulations:

The Forest Service viewed the publicizing of special regulations authorized in section 10 of the Act as optional until the Duck Creek timber sale decision. This supposition was based on the "as he deems necessary" language in that section. Presumably "he" refers to a district ranger. In the opinion of the Forest Service, existing regulations were adequate and special regulations, other than private land regulations, were not necessary.

Evans believes the Forest Service has never wanted to treat Hells Canyon as a special place. He concedes their "public relations" portrays it differently, but on the ground actions speak louder. Evans says the Forest Service manages the canyon like any other ranger district.

He is especially critical of the Forest Service's new emphasis on "public safety" logging – the continuation of amendments and exceptions to the management plan which sanctions the taking of large and old "hazard trees" near campgrounds and trail heads.

"Take a look at the Upper Imnaha and how it has been trashed by the logging of more than just a few 'hazard trees.' In 2014 there was a huge log deck piled next to the entrance of a campground. The number of hazard trees as they euphemistically call them all but destroyed the ambiance of the original campground."

"Had the National Park Service been managing the canyon, this never would have happened," he added caustically.

Draft private land use regulations were included in the comprehensive management plan, but this document was held up in appeals until 1984. By then, much had changed, such as the addition of wilderness acres and local county planning and zoning. It was necessary to do an extensive rewrite. Progress, however, ground to a halt under direction from the Reagan Administration to not promulgate new federal regulations. In 1991, work resumed on the private land use regulations. The draft was extensively rewritten and a series of public reviews held. The final regulations for private lands within the National Recreation Area were published on June 13, 1994.

Interim rules for management of national forest lands were published in the Federal Register and became effective on October 5, 1989. The final rules were adopted on July 19, 1994. In these rules, the agency gave itself authority to regulate any type of river craft, an authority it attempted to get Congress to provide in the Hells Canyon Act. Congress refused.

The Hells Canyon Alliance (a largely power-boat funded organization put together by Sandra Mitchell) pointed out this apparent conflict with congressional intent in its comments on the regulations. While other reactions by the Alliance were recognized in the final regulations and resulted in some changes, this comment was not addressed. (See appendix for copy of PL-94, -199).

SANDRA MITCHELL & THE HELLS CANYON ALLIANCE

THE MODERN DAY Hells Canyon story has a heroine without whom entry into the fray would have resulted in power boats banned, hunting prohibited, and surrounding environs declared a national park.

By all accounts she just may be the reincarnation of former First District Congresswoman Gracie Pfost – the original "Hells' Belle" of Hells Canyon. Those that may disagree do so on the basis of believing the latter version of Hells' Belle is tougher and smarter than Ms. Pfost.

Sandra Mitchell was the talented and tenacious director of public lands for the Idaho Snow Machine Association and the Idaho Recreation Council. She is the heart and soul of a sizable segment of the Idaho electorate – those that enjoy the backcountry riding on ATV designated trails or snowmobiling in the backcountry.

Depending on one's perspective, Mitchell is either an angel or the devil incarnate. Regardless, she is a masterful tactician with a solid command of the issues. Evans, who has high regard for Mitchell, believes she does an excellent job raising funds from snowmobile manufacturers, ATV companies, firearms and ammunition firms, hunting and sportsman groups and others which financially depend on access to public lands.

Various polls indicate a solid majority of Idahoans prefer to access the back country on ATVs or snowmobiles, depending on the season. For these outdoor recreationists, Mitchell is their champion and she is directly employed by Joe Scott, grandson of Joe Albertson, founder of the grocery store chain.

Scott has several loves: 1) He strongly supports educational reform in Idaho and through the Albertson Foundation has spent millions aiding the badly underfunded public school sector. 2) He loves the Idaho outdoors and enjoys accessing the backcountry on ATVs or dirt bikes or snowmobiles.

The primary issue in conflict between the Hells Canyon Alliance and the Hells Canyon Preservation Council is that of noise. Many conservationists believe that a special aspect of the wilderness experience is being away from machine generated noise. The philosophy contained within the 1964 Wilderness Act makes it clear man is a temporary visitor to a wilderness area and should neither leave a trace of his presence nor generate noise that detracts from another's experience.

Other than planes that utilize the back country air strips grandfathered into the Wilderness Act, the Forest Service when clearing trails in wilderness areas cannot utilize chain saws. Trail crews use old fashioned cross cuts.

Many outdoor recreationists chafe at these restrictions and would, if they could, amend the original act and liberalize the language.

In Hells Canyon, the issue devolved into a dispute between those that liked to float the Snake and enjoy a wilderness experience without having to hear jet boats, and those who believe jet boats or other mechanized craft, on water and land, have always been a part of the canyon experience.

Brock Evans correctly points out that the multiple-use recreationists most often refer to members of environmental groups as "posey-sniffin' tree-huggers," or utilize pejorative tags such as "elitist" and "purists." He further contends the Sierra Club has never proposed banning all man-made noise as critics charge and readily recognize economics will never have passenger jets flying around national parks and wilderness areas. While they may not like man-made noises that penetrate into one's wilderness experience, most are realists.

Evans dismisses a term like "purist," pointing out it is nothing more than a demeaning code word charging environmentalists with being selfish.

"True enough, we can't stand the noise of a machine, raucous or not, in an area where we go to experience and enjoy solitude and quiet."

He points out also that many multiple-use recreationists appear to love the sound of loud boats and cites jet boat races that annually race on parts of the Salmon, the Snake and the St. Joe Rivers.

"We try to avoid name-calling and to stick to facts. We describe what our critics do and how it adversely can impact water and land."

Evans recognizes that a jet boat trip up and down the canyon from Lewiston to Sheep Creek is a valid but different kind of out-door experience than a three-day float trip. He says there is room for both, and, as of this writing so does the U.S. Forest Service.

Joe Scott's recognition that Sandra Mitchell might well be the answer to his prayers was fortuitous. He pays her well, but she delivers. When she and Scott stumbled onto the fact that HCPC's Ric Bailey was campaigning for a national park designation, they sprang into action.

Rightly or wrongly, they felt a national park would result in the banning of jet boats not to mention motorized craft in the canyon, as well as a ban on hunting.

Evans says that while the issues of hunting and noise from jet boats are concerning, the issue that drove Bailey to campaign for a national park was to transfer management of the NRA from the Forest Service to the National Park Service.

"The main issue for Ric and us was not the jet

boats, but rather the Forest Service's mindset, especially their utter inability to stop logging, or whatever other misleading code-phrase they come up with to justify the unjustifiable. They are totally incapable of breaking out of their historic mold," says Evans.

He also disagreed with Governor Andrus and Senator McClure regarding the continuation of any kind of logging within the NRA. "In my experience sustained-yield selective logging is just another one of the code-phrases used by the Forest Service and its logging allies," he states, adding, "for those of us in the environmental network, selective logging simply means select a forest and log it all."

Mitchell proved to be a tough and tenacious opponent. She honed her skills working in Republican campaigns and then serving as a district representative for Congressman and later Senator Steve Symms. She was an apt learner with the ability to absorb massive detail, condense it and put it in words the average Idahoan could understand.

Born in Klamath Falls, Oregon, in 1947, Mitchell migrated with her family to the Tri-Cities in the early 50s largely because there was work to be obtained in the federal government's development of the Hanford Nuclear complex.

During her time there, she said the family lived in all three of the Tri-Cities at different times: Pasco, Kennewick and Richland. The summer after the ninth grade, the family moved to Ketchikan, Alaska.

Neither she nor her brother were fond of Ketchikan, and soon after she graduated from high school in 1965, she headed to the University of Wyoming. She later told an interviewer she thought she was going to freeze to death. She had not realized the town and the university were located at over 7,000 feet.

Following that freshman year, she transferred to

the University of Idaho. Midway through her junior year, however, she married Chuck Gabby, Jr., who had a wheat ranch near Lewiston.

She quickly realized she had married into one of the leading Republican families in the county and she began to pay attention to politics and *The Lewiston Morning Tribune*. She found the newspaper to be far more liberal on its editorial pages than she was. Her father-in-law, Chuck Gabby, Sr., had served as the Republican county chairman and her mother-in-law was also active in GOP politics.

In 1976, she read a *Tribune* story that indicated the Nez Perce County Republican Central Committee was bringing Arizona Senator Barry Goldwater, one of her political heroes, to Lewiston for a speech. She called Republican headquarters to volunteer, was assigned to ticket sales, and was hooked.

Not even the former 1964 Republican presidential candidate canceling at the last minute diminished her enthusiasm. Barry Goldwater, Jr., the son and a former California congressman, came in his place and the event was a success.

In 1977 she became the volunteer Nez Perce County coordinator for Congressman Steve Symms re-election campaign, which Symms easily won. Symms then began to prepare his campaign to knock off Senator Frank Church in the 1980 election cycle.

Sometime in the late 70s, Mitchell was introduced to Lewiston businessman Rich Rodgers, who would have a profound influence on her future. Rodgers owned the Toyota/Subaru/Dodge/Jeep dealership in Lewiston. He was good friends with Mitchell's second husband, John Church, who owned a thriving farm implement and machinery business.

When Rodgers found out that another of his good friends, Albertson heir Joe Scott, was looking for a government affairs person to lobby Congress and the Idaho Legislature to keep public lands open to ATVs and snowmobiles, Rodgers sent a letter endorsing Mitchell.

Protecting the rights of jet boaters to their usual and accustomed practices in the canyon quickly became Mitchell's priority.

While Mitchell followed the fight surrounding the original passage of the bill, largely written by Frank Church and Jim McClure, creating the original Hells Canyon National Recreation Area, she did not engage in the fight over the National Park designation until going to work for Joe Scott in 1992.

She was drawn into the fight by its members in the Idaho Snow Machine Association. Many owned jet boats and enjoyed boating up the canyon gorge. A charismatic former logging truck driver, Ric Bailey, had taken over the Hells Canyon Preservation Council in the early 90s. By then, it had become a moribund organization. He was revitalizing the group to support his vision, and the vision of many members of the environmental community, that Hells Canyon be re-designated a national park.

This proposal encountered fierce opposition from the jet boat community and the hundreds of thousands of Idahoans who owned fishing and hunting licenses.

Evans believes this issue could have been handled satisfactorily through negotiations and that it was not a make-or-break matter for most canyon park proponents.

Additionally, Governor Andrus and Senator McClure believed there were some drainages that would tolerate selective logging on a sustained-yield basis and thus maintain the viability of several saw mills in the region.

The two also believed conferring national parks status on Hells Canyon would lead the area to be loved to death by too many tourists, creating a situation similar to the overcrowding occurring in California's Yosemite

National Park.

The surrogate fight in this struggle became a battle over noise between those that like to raft through the canyon and those who wanted to use their boats.

Mitchell became the champion of the jet boat folks and Bailey the hero of the Sierra Club and the Save Our Salmon groups who wanted only non-motorized craft in the wild and scenic portion of the canyon.

Mitchell is one of those skilled lobbyists who knows she has to master and to explain her opponent's main arguments, as well as articulate the positions of the groups she represents. She, like Evans, does her homework. She loves to read and research. Rare is a member of Congress or the Idaho Legislature who knows more than she does.

The one person who was invaluable to her efforts and one with whom she readily insists shared equally in her success was Art Seamans. Mitchell accepted her position with Joe Scott in May 1992. Seamans came on board a couple of months later in a part-time position. He had retired from the Wallowa-Whitman National Forest in early 1992. He had transferred from the Nez Perce National Forest as the Moose Creek Ranger in 1980 and

Sandra Mitchell, leader of the Hells Canyon Alliance and the savior of keeping jet boats operating in the NRA. She knew Senator Church intended jet boats to be grandfathered into legislation given their historic use. Photo: Sandra Mitchell

had served as assistant river manager and then River Manager of the Wild and Scenic Snake River. After his retirement, he worked part-time for Scott.

Mitchell states unequivocally that, "Art was probably the smartest man I have ever met! It was a privilege to know him and a joy to have had the opportunity to work with him. He did a great deal of the research and because he knew the river so well and lived through the previous planning process, he was an amazing asset."

Seamans also worked on the other OHV/OSV boating issues. He handled a good deal of the technical work because he understood the workings of the Forest Service.

As pointed out earlier, if one includes the steam wheelers that plied the Snake River from Lewiston starting in the 1880s, Hells Canyon has a long history of motorized boating. It was not until the jet boat was perfected in the early 1950s, however, that motorized traffic exploded. Conflict between the jet boaters and those that liked to float on rafts or take kayaks though the canyon was inevitable. What was not devined was the skillful manner in which Mitchell was able to protect her interest group and most of what they sought.

A brief history of boating in Hells Canyon is in order. There exists a rich tradition of power boating that spans more than a century.

In 1865, Captain Tom Stump took the 110-foot *Colonel Wright* up river into what is now the Hells Canyon National Recreation Area (HCNRA). He turned around at a point 25 miles above where the Salmon River flows into the Snake River. In 1870, Captain Sebastian Miller brought the 136-foot steamboat *Shoshone* from southern Idaho to Lewiston. In 1895, Captain William Gray followed the route blazed by Bas Miller in the *Norma*, a 165-foot stern wheeler. The steamer *Imnaha* ferried supplies to

Sandra Mitchell & the Hells Canyon Alliance

Scenic view of Snake River as seen from river trail.

the Eureka Bar mine and mill site in 1903, followed by the *Mountain Gem* in 1904. All of this history can be found in Cort Conley's book, *Snake River in Hells Canyon*.

As his book points out, the many homesteaders and miners who called the Hells Canyon home in the early 1900s needed transportation. The Snake River was a ready highway, just as the St. Joe, the Clearwater, the Salmon, the Lochsa, the Selway and the Coeur d'Alene Rivers were some of the first "highways" one followed into Idaho's frontier interior.

One of the first to provide commercial boat service on the navigable Snake River was Ed MacFarlane in 1910 with his 36-foot gasoline powered *Flyer*. Two years later he added the 65-foot *Prospector* to his fleet. MacFarlane began the first power boat tour business operating out of the Lewiston area, charging $1.50 for a trip to Wild Goose Rapids.

In 1914, he braved those rapids to Granite Creek with 19 passengers. Many boat captains and craft took their place in the traditions and history of the canyon over the years. These include characters of legendary dimensions, such as Press Brewrink, Kyle McGrady, Oliver McNabb and Dick Rivers. Their large and sturdy propeller driven craft included names like the *Chief Joseph, Let's Go, Clipper, Idaho, Florence, Wenaha* and *Idaho Queen.*

    The first Snake River mail delivery contract was awarded to Press Brewrink in 1919. Weekly deliveries from Lewiston to Johnson Bar continues today, operated by Beamer's. The boat goes up on Wednesday and returns on Thursday, providing a valuable service for canyon residents. The night is usually spent at a cabin that Beamer's operates on the Oregon side of the river near Dug Bar.

    For tourists the ride up river into Hells Canyon on the mail boat is an adventure. Those who recall the opening chapter of Grace Jordan's book, *Home Below Hells Canyon*, know that it starts off with Grace and the family boarding the mail boat to head for their new home in the early 1930s at Kirkwood Bar.

    As mentioned earlier, a New Zealand sheep rancher named Bill Hamilton revolutionized river running with the first practical, jet-propelled boat in 1954. This miraculous craft could operate in shallow water and proved a match for some of New Zealand's toughest white water.

    Boats with jet pumps first appeared on the U.S. scene in the late 50's. Norm Riddle, a jet boat pioneer, says Jim West was one of the first to use a jet boat in Hells Canyon, employing a fiberglass and wood craft with a Beuhler pump. In 1962, Bob Smith and Paul Filer took a welded aluminum boat with twin outboards up river through Hells Canyon to Oxbow and returned in one day. After the completion of Idaho Power's Hells Canyon Dam, in 1968 this trip was no longer possible,

    Riddle began running jet boats into the canyon in 1963. He notes it was rare to see rafts at that time. In 1965,

Norm married tough welded aluminum hulls and the jet pump, producing a craft that could run through shallows and rapids, was light but tough enough to withstand the rigors of white water. While early designs were crude and utilitarian, they evolved into the efficient craft we have today, boats, engines and pumps capable of safely running all of Hells Canyon's rapids yet handsome enough to appeal to family boat buyers.

Rick Ripley, former editorial page editor of the *Idaho Statesman* and former publisher of Spokane's *Business Journal*, and a great fishing and hiking companion, recently published a book (*Against the Torrents*, Backeddy Press, 2016) on the Bentz brothers, Darell and Rusty, who also played a significant role perfecting jet boats.

Two industries grew from these pioneer efforts – jet boat manufacturing (Lewiston/Clarkston Valley has 13 such companies) and tourism.

Nineteen outfitters today carry 20,000 people annually in power boats, a vital part of the region's tourist industry. Of course there are many other businesses and services that support power boating: marine engines, upholstery and tops, jet pumps, fuel, hotels, restaurants, etc.

Use of the river through Hells Canyon by those who like to float also has a long and distinguished history. The first European-American to float the length of the canyon, Donald McKenzie, made his amazing journey in 1819.

During the late 1800's several boaters penetrated the canyon to various degrees, investigating the river's potential for navigation and assessing its mineral resources, real and imagined. In 1925, a young adventurer named Amos Burg traversed the canyon with a canoe. He returned to Hells Canyon on three other occasions, the first with a canoe in 1929, the second by raft in 1946 and

Historic sign at Dug Bar where the Nez Perce forded the Snake in 1877 while heading to Canada ahead of U.S. Army troops commanded by one-armed Civil War hero, General Oliver Howard. Photo: Marcia Carlson

third by raft in 1978.

Five parties left accounts of floating the river in the 1940s, including one outfitter trip. Surplus rafts from World War II made river running more available and inexpensive. By the 1950s and 1960s, more people were braving the rapids of the Northwest's rivers, including Hells Canyon, but it wasn't until the early 1970s that float use exploded.

The definition for a "Wild and Scenic River" calls for essentially primitive and undeveloped shorelines. The Snake River in Hells Canyon doesn't perfectly fit the preferred definition. With three dams up stream that trap sediment, for example, the numerous sandy beaches have largely disappeared.

Flows are controlled by the dams and can change hourly. Even the river channel itself has been heavily modified over a long span of time to enhance navigation by the large, deeper draft craft that used to ply the river for commerce. The river canyon at the turn of the 20th century was lined with ranches and farms, now mostly abandoned.

Over 2,000 people once occupied the Oregon side of the canyon alone in the early 1900s; more worked lands on the Idaho side. There were towns, schools, wagon roads, irrigation ditches, orchards, fields and other features of civilization, many still visible today, even in the Hells Canyon Wilderness. With the help of nature, the Forest Service has embarked on a process of re-creating a wilderness area, but successful as it may appear, once it is gone, it is gone.

The first reference to modification of the river channel in Hells Canyon appears in a 1903 *Lewiston Tribune* article which relates a trip by the steamboat *Imnaha* with a party of government engineers who would blast away the large rock that obstructed navigation at the Mountain Sheep Rapid.

In 1914, according to Cort Conley's book, $25,000 was appropriated by Congress for the Corps of Engineers to improve the river channel with explosives. From 1903 until designation under the Wild and Scenic Rivers Act in 1975, the Corps of Engineers continued projects to improve navigation of the Snake River in what is now Hells Canyon. This included blasting rocks, construction of diversions to channel water and installation of channel navigation aids from Lewiston to the end of navigation improvements, 86 miles up-river. The balance of the river to Hells Canyon Dam (18 miles) is without survey markers.

LEGISLATION: FACTS TO JUSTIFY REGS

NO MATTER HOW one slices and dices the use numbers on an annual basis, the empirical evidence shows jet boats provide ten times as many people the opportunity to experience the canyon as compared to those who float the river.

The numbers became more than good guesstimates with the opening of the Cache Creek public contact station at the north end of the river in the spring of 1991. Up to that time, compliance with the permit system by upstream traveling power boaters entering the HCNRA had been minimal; enforcement also was rare to nonexistent. An apparent surge in 1991 jet boat use actually reflected the improved rate of compliance.

During the 1992 regulated season, 12,168 individuals floated in the HCNRA. This includes floaters launching below Hells Canyon Dam, below Rush Creek, and from the Lower Salmon. During this same period, 23,220 people accessed the HCNRA by power boat, 2 of every 3 visitors. If only Snake River rafters are considered, power boaters comprise 81% of the total, 5,556 versus 23,220 power boaters. Much of the boat use took place in unrestricted sections of the river below Rush Creek.

When annual figures are considered, power boating dominates river use even more. Commercial power boaters brought 27,230 people into the HCNRA in 1992 (92% of the total commercial passengers) for 31,731 service days. This compares with 2,516 Hells Canyon commercial float passengers for 6,815 service days.

The numbers for 2015 actually show a decline in commercial canyon float trips with only 1,365 passengers being taken through the canyon by commercial float trip companies. This number translates into 5,730 service days.

In 2015, the total number of visitors to and through the canyon was 25,225. This number is slightly below the average for visitors during the previous decade. If the four lower Snake dams are ever, in effect removed, the number can be expected to drop dramatically for many of the visitors to the canyon come to Lewiston on small cruise ships which offer the day trip up and into Hells Canyon as an extra excursion. Without slack water, those ships would vanish.

These numbers more than justify the HCA's adamant stance against proposals such as alternating days of the week between the floaters and the jet boaters. Likewise, the heavy preponderance of power boats also reflects hunters coming into the canyon in search of chukars, deer and elk. Were Hells Canyon proclaimed a National Park, this hunting would not be allowed unless "park preserves" were created.

HCA believes any significant change in management of the Snake River in the HCNRA that reduces access by powered craft will have impacts that reverberate through the surrounding communities. The most obvious effects will be to the 19 commercial outfitters who make their livings, taking passengers into the canyon. Ancillary industries would also be damaged.

A rough and conservative estimate done in 1993 of the economic impact of power boating in todays dollars came to nearly $40 million annually.

University of Idaho Study:

In preparation for the management plan review the Forest Service surveyed people who use the river. The study, contracted with the University of Idaho, was designed to provide information about river users: who they are, how they use the river, their perceptions of the river and management preferences. The study segregated data by different boater groups – commercial float, private float, commercial power and private power. It ran from April 15, 1988 through April 14, 1989. The University mailed 1,927 questionnaires and received a 77% return rate.

The study is more remarkable for the group similarities it disclosed than the differences. All took river trips for the same reasons, to be close to nature, enjoy the white water, to be with family and friends, for excitement and to visit wild lands. While discussions about crowding absorbed much of the task force's time during the limits of acceptable change (LAC) effort, the study showed that 65% of respondents did not feel crowded. Concerns by the 35% that did experience some crowding were concentrated on one section of river and focused, to a large extent, on campsite issues. Only 24% had negative contacts with other groups; complaints focused on camp conflicts and rudeness.

In the problem identification section of the study, responses between groups were so close that they were aggregated for analysis. Most boaters didn't encounter the problems listed; fewer than 25% identified any item as a minor or major problem. Over 80% of respondents from all groups wanted to maintain the existing experience.

Reactions to different management actions and facilities options were mixed. The bottom line, however, is located in the study report's conclusion. On a scale from 1 to 10, where 1 is the worst trip ever and 10 is the best trip ever, 68% ranked their experience an 8 or above. Only 1% called it a 1, 2, or 3.

The Hells Canyon Alliance:

The Hells Canyon Alliance, formed by Sandra Mitchell in 1994, provides a common voice for those who supported shared use of the Wild and Scenic Snake River in the Hells Canyon National Recreation Area. During the Forest Service's management planning process, Mitchell and her cohorts found that their voices often went unheard or weren't taken seriously. She believes the Forest Service listened more to the environmentalists rather than the interests she represents. Of course, Evans insists it was the other way around. Only by working together and pooling resources was the alliance able to become an effective force.

The HCA represented a broad spectrum of citizens, businesses and organizations, many of whom had first-hand experience in Hells Canyon. The original founding organizations were the Northwest Power Boat Association, Western White Water Association, and River Access for Tomorrow (RAFT). The alliance was soon joined by: Adventures Afloat, Anderson River Adventures, Beamers Hells Canyon Tours and Excursions, Bentz Boats, Cougar Country Lodge, Inc., Foundation for North American Wild Sheep, Hells Canyon Adventures II, Inc., Hells Canyon Challenge, Inc., Idaho Sportsmen's Coalition, Intermountain Excursions, Leo-Tek Manufacturing, Lewis-Clark Economic Development Assoc., Lewiston Chamber of Commerce, Mainstream Outdoor Adventures, Meyer's Outfitting, Northwest Timber Workers Resource Council, Peer's Snake River Rafting, Red Woods Outfitters, Riddle Marine, River Adventures, Ltd., Riverview Marina, Snake Dancer Excursions, Snake River Adventures, Snake River Outfitters, Steen's Wilderness Adventures, Welded Aluminum Boat Manufacturers Association, and Z & S Outfitters, Inc.

That funding power made the HCA an effective player in Hells Canyon. Its Board of Directors included a broad spectrum of those concerned with Hells Canyon's future: rafters and power boaters (both commercial and private), boat manufacturers and business people.

Legislation: Facts to Justify Regs

They assembled an outstanding team, captained by Executive Director Mitchell, and including a recreation specialist and attorneys all with political experience in environmental law and its application or misapplication.

Not to minimize the issue, but there are clear differences involved with the modes of transportation in Hells Canyon in the ways jet boaters and rafters recreate:

- Power boaters spend less time on lands along the river than rafters during the summer's regulated season. Most of the power boaters' activities are water based. While some camp along the river, the majority are day users. Much of their land activity takes place at hardened sites such as the Kirkwood Historic Ranch. Most rafters camp along the river and spend relatively little time on the water (2.5 -3 hours) each day. The balance of their time is spent in camp, scouting rapids and taking side trips.
- Regulated season power boaters who do camp stay less time than rafters. The average length of stay for all power boaters is 1.3 days, versus 2.4 days for rafters. Power boaters who camp have smaller parties: 3 people average per private power boat party compared to 9 people for private float parties.
- Float craft are rarely seen during this time except immediately before and after the control period. The single largest draw for power boating during the unregulated season is steelhead fishing. This is primarily a water-based, day-use activity with no land impact. Big game hunting draws fewer people, but most of them do camp along the river and hike into the mid-elevation benches. Little of their time is spent in the corridor; the game they hunt is much higher on the canyon face. Chukar hunting is a day use activity.
- A few private power boaters camp between

Wild Sheep Rapid and Rush Creek Rapid, the section of river with the fewest campsites. The reason is simple: Most don't want to run the big rapids with a load of camping gear. Rafters nearly always have to camp in this section of river. The limit placed on control period float launches is based on the numbers of campsites in the first two days of a float trip, Hells Canyon Dam to Rush Creek. Power boater competition with rafters for camp sites is not much of a factor on this section of river. However, conflict over campsites could be completely eliminated if the Forest Service would implement a campsite reservation system established in 1983 by the Department of Agriculture.

- Most power boaters who camp set up their equipment at one site and stay there for the duration of the visit. Rafters usually stay one night at each site, setting up new camps every night.
- Power boaters have superior mobility and can go up or down river to locate a suitable campsite. Rafters are on a one way trip and finding a suitable campsites can become a consuming task that ruins an otherwise enjoyable experience. There conflicts could be easily managed with a reservation system.
- Almost half (47%) of the float trips at Pittsburg landing. Another 24% terminated above Pittsburg and jet boated back to Hells Canyon Dam. Only 19% went all of the way through the HCNRA to the Grande Ronde. Floating is concentrated in the 31.5 miles of wild river above Pittsburg Landing.
- Much of the private power boat use takes place between the HCNRA's north boundary and the Salmon River, an area visited by only 19% of the Hells Canyon rafters. The bulk of the upstream commercial day use trips turn around below Rush Creek.

Legislation: Facts to Justify Regs

USFS Management Plans:

That a recreation management plan was needed for the Snake River and Hells Canyon first dawned on the Forest Service in 1973. The area was then managed as part of the Hells Canyon-Seven Devils Scenic Area. While the Forest Service had a jet boat patrol on the river, its use was limited to cleanup work and administrative transportation for fire, trail and range crews.

According to Mitchell, a float outfitter asked the three forest supervisors involved in managing the scenic area and their district rangers to accompany him on a float trip. He worked diligently to show them that raft use had grown to a point that it was out of control and a threat to the area's resources. Power boating was not even an issue. He was successful in his quest and convinced the Forest Services leaders to impose a moratorium on issuance of any new float outfitter permits. There were 18 permits processed at that time and many more awaiting a decision. Private float use, like power boating, was not a major player in the growing use impact picture at that juncture. Once the moratorium was imposed, the permitted businesses instantly acquired a value they did not previously possess. The host outfitter who promoted the moratorium so successfully later sold his two Hells Canyon businesses.

As a result of the float trip and other complaints from outfitters about crowding at the launch facility and up-river campsites, the supervisors also initiated work on a management plan focused on floating, the element of river use threatening to get completely out of hand. The first plan was completed in 1975, adopting the moratorium and setting a target of 16 float businesses with one launch every 8 days.

Most floats at that time were 6 days in length, going to the Grande Ronde takeout. A limit of 5 launches from points between Hells Canyon Dam and Rush Creek would be allowed each day during a control season, 3 private and 2 commercial as soon as the target of 16 permits was reached.

Prior to that, the extra two businesses were accommodated with three commercial and two private launches on some days. Non-use of some permits allowed achievement of the targeted sixteen in short order. This worked out to a 50/50 allocation between commercial and private boats in terms of numbers of people because of the larger commercial party size. For float folks the limit of five launches per day was based on the campsite availability in the first two days of the average trip and the capacity of the launch ramp at Hells Canyon Creek. These limitations are still valid and were not questioned during the recent management plan review.

The Interim Plan

In December 1975 the Hells Canyon National Recreation Area was designated by legislation sponsored by Idaho senators Frank Church and Jim McClure, and was promptly signed by then President Gerald Ford. The legislation called for completion of a comprehensive management plan (CMP) by December, 1980.

A planning team was assembled by the Forest Service and began its task in 1976. An interim management plan was approved for the river, adopting, in large, a 1975 plan. Commercial power boat businesses were to be placed under special use permit and a first-come, first-served system was adopted for private float authorizations and reservations.

Nothing makes bureaucrats happier than putting together comprehensive management plans (CMP). They supposedly represent the best input with all views considered, with interest groups and the public given plenty of opportunity to weigh in. The "superior path" selected, reviewed by a gaggle of lawyers and given Holy

Legislation: Facts to Justify Regs

Grail status.

When the Hells Canyon CMP was near completion, it underwent another internal review by the head of the Forest Service Chief by Acting Deputy Chief R. M. Housley sent a moratorium to the regional forester on July 10, 1980, directing changes. Housley wanted further justification for the continued use of power boats on the wild portion of the river, the very heart of Hells Canyon. He wrote: "The proposed level of use is so low it appears that now may be a good time to eliminate all power boat use. If use becomes established under this plan it will be extremely difficult to eliminate it in the future."

This memorandum clearly communicated the direction from upper management to eliminate power boats from the heart of Hells Canyon – if not now, then later.

This came in spite of a stated willingness by the planning team to listen to all users without prejudice. It encouraged rafters and power boaters to compromise and propose an alternative for shared use with limits numbers. The team did so, but the alternative was discarded. It may be that Forest Service planners were not even aware of the memo's existence. The upper level tinkering resulting in the plan's power boat closure, as directed by Housley, took place in the regional office.

The ultimate irony is the easiest way to have brought forth a ban about would have been legislation designating the NRA as a unit of the National Park Service, thereby guaranteeing the area's future as a true wilderness.

The planning team finished its task and a management plan was sent to the regional forester and the Forest Service in December 1980. Max Peterson, Forest Service chief, signed the plan on May 23, 1981, and must have felt as if he had just slid down a banister of razor blades. A feature of the plan was a full control period closing the wild river from Wild Sheep Rapid to Rush Creek Rapid to power boats. This resulted in over 20 appeals from outraged power boaters who had worked out a compromise with rafters to limit power boat access in that section of river but not eliminate it.

Senators McClure and Steve Symms and Congressman Larry Craig sent a letter to Peterson, on July 15, 1981, challenging the plan, asserting that it failed to comply with the letter and intent of the Act. They asked him to withdraw his decision. In an unprecedented move, the Forest Service chief did just that. He appointed a committee to review the plan and make recommendations. The committee advised him to allow power boat access on the entire river, but to limit numbers during the control period in the upper section, a proposal close to the original power/float compromise. It was at this point that the Housley memo surfaced. Local managers said they had no knowledge of the memo's existence.

Peterson signed his second decision, adopting the new committee's recommendation on May 12, 1982. As one might expect, relationships between the Forest Service and the power boaters were wounded by what they saw as a betrayal of trust.

They decided to fight any restrictions on their access and more appeals were filed against the second plan than the first. It is worth pointing out that at no time did float interests enter the process, either in support or against the Forest Service. They left the agency swinging in the wind alone on a gallows of its own construction.

In fact, the Forest Service had failed to establish that power boat use in this segment of river was at a level requiring restrictions to meet any defined goals or objectives. It wasn't challenged on its float allocation because physical factors dictated the limit. In the case of power boating, however, any limits had to be based

Legislation: Facts to Justify Regs

on resource concerns, social factors or experience objectives. Nothing in the plan supported limits based on them.

Nevertheless, on April 21, 1983, Assistant Secretary of Agriculture John Crowell signed a decision on the river management portion of the CMP. His determination for the balance of the plan didn't come until April 1984. Crowell placed no limits on day-use by power boats, but did require assignment of campsites, a directive never implemented.

Campsite assignments would have resolved most of the conflicts being experienced in the canyon. They would have imposed an indirect limit on power boat overnight use, as well. Crowell called for continued registration of all boaters and monitoring of the effects of boat use on other values. If the Forest Service determined that adjustments to boating use levels were necessary, it could do so, but not before the 1985 season and only after giving notice and soliciting public involvement.

This became a critical preservationist long-term policy objective and it fell under the euphemistic phrase "limits of acceptable change" (LAC). The Forest Service would monitor conditions along the river corridor and, in response to a perceived increase in boating activity throughout the river's length, would note everything from more dust in the air to more mud in the river or smoke in the air.

Students from the University of Idaho were hired and charged with data collection on during the 1988 and 1989 seasons. This study also monitored social conditions overlooked in the original CMP.

For example, the Forest Service would hire a college student from Idaho's School of Natural Resources, and pay him or her to sleep the dirt landing strip next to Dug Bar. Every time a plane landed, the student was to note how much dust was raised and guess how much of it was carried into the Snake by the wind. This would be added to other data and someone somewhere had a pre-constructed formula defining how much carrying capacity the river had and its ability to absorb this dust.

Of course, one had to set aside the fluctuating levels of water as the dam operators managed the outflow from the Hells Canyon Dam with maximum power generation in mind.

The unspoken goal was to establish a basis to justify closing off back country air strips despite being explicitly grandfathered into the Wilderness Act of 1964. The prime sponsor was Idaho Senator Frank Church who knew what he was dealing with at the USFS and knew the need to restrict its problematic instruments.

A review of the river management portion of the comprehensive management plan, utilizing the limits of acceptable change process, began in 1990. A twenty-two member task force met nineteen times over twenty-two months and, after two hundred and fifty hours of work, hammered out a compromise, recommending river management plan based on goals and objectives. This task force consisted of representatives from all interest groups and was facilitated by the University of Idaho. The recommended plan included limits for power boaters and rafters in the wild river. The premise was that desired conditions are defined and standards established. When monitoring shows these standards are about to be exceeded, various management actions are implemented, such as education or site hardening. When all else fails, regulations come into play.

The final acceptable change report was issued in September 1991 with only two task force members dissenting.

The next step in modification of the CMP was completion of an environmental impact statement. The Forest Service began that process in the fall of 1992 with

Legislation: Facts to Justify Regs

a series of meetings for scoping and issue development. The recommendation was presented as a proposed alternative. Initially, the Forest Service had hoped that an environmental assessment would suffice and that it could be implemented by spring of 1993. It became evident that a full-blown environmental impact statement would be prudent if not mandatory.

On August 11, 1993, a draft statement was released. The years of effort, intensive public involvement, and hours of negotiation represented by the limits of acceptable change plan were abandoned in favor of a scheme that the acceptable change task force had considered and rejected as unworkable.

As a preferred alternative, the Wallowa-Whitman Forest supervisor decided to allow rafters exclusive access to the wild river one week, and power boaters the next. Power boat launches were severely limited. In spite of overwhelming public support for shared use, incompatibility between rafters and power boaters was cited as the reason for this restriction.

The public reaction was massive and unanimously against the plan which would essentially halve everyone's access to the wild river. Some 75% of the public input supported the limits of acceptable change solution with some adjustments for faulty data.

The final environmental impact statement was released on August 11, 1994, conjuring up a worse plan for most of Hells Canyon's boaters than the draft every-other-week proposal. Basically, and in spite of testimony to the contrary, the Forest Service decided noise indeed was a key wilderness value and there was going to be a compromise in which, during the summer, there were some days of the week in which those floating the canyon could look forward to a noise-free time.

Power boaters were eliminated from the heart of Hells Canyon for three days a week in July and August to provide a near-wilderness experience for floaters. The Forest Service conceded that the plan was based on social, not resource, concerns. An opportunity was given for further input of new information, and massive amounts of data were submitted. Mitchell believes, though, qualifiers placed on the nature of the input assured that most of it would be disregarded.

On November 9, 1994, the final plan was made public with only minor changes. The Hells Canyon Alliance, three pilot's associations, two state agencies, four environmental organizations, three individuals and eighteen of the nineteen commercial power boaters, appealed. Upon review, the regional forester granted a stay, delaying enforcement of the plan until September 15, 1995.

Appeal decisions began showing up on July 20, 1995. Part of the plan was to be implemented in September 1995 after the stay was lifted, a few items were dumped and the rest was sent back to planning. Those things affirmed by the decision, such as removal of picnic tables, pit toilets and navigational markers in the wild river section, were to happen with lifting of the stay.

Everything not affirmed or reversed was returned for more analysis. The issues concerning numbers for commercial power boaters were to be given further study and the planning process was to be undertaken by the Wallowa-Whitman National Forest with some sort of oversight by the Regional Office.

There were two areas of special concern to power boaters. First, the regional forester upheld use of visitor data from 1988-1992. Those numbers were flawed and inaccurate for private use, based on guesses of compliance. They do not provide a clear picture of the canyon usage and no amount of review would provide accurate data; it simply doesn't exist. Second, the concept of a non-motorized window was upheld. However, the exact timing and duration was to be studied.

Other plan features that Deputy Regional Forester Richard Ferraro affirmed include:
- the supervisor correctly followed the process
- outfitter-guide services are needed
- the supervisor chose a fair allocation system
- the prohibiting the cutting or burning of live or dead vegetation
- implementing a chainsaw ban
- establishing "user etiquette" education
- limiting party size for noncommercial users
- limiting maximum private float craft per party
- establishing campsite stay limits
- the establishment of a "no-wake" zone at administrative and developed recreation sites
- prohibiting personal motorized water craft, such as jet skis

Among those items "affirmed with direction" included:
- setting of commercial capacity based on the highest 2 out of 5 years (1988-1992), modified by the five-year average. A required review of actual use records for those years and verification or refinement of the cap estimate;
- The forest supervisor also supported the carrying capacities established in the plan, but delayed limitations beyond those currently in effect until a permit-by-permit analysis for commercial uses is completed.

He reversed the following:
- the supervisor must further analyze specific effects of allocation and operational limitations on individual permits
- the supervisor must conduct further analysis of

private land access
- aircraft access restrictions, including seaplanes
- the direction to eliminate drop camps and establish hours of operation.

This latter item reflected that the USFS was hell bent on over-managing power boats, outfitters and guides. In September 1995, the Wallowa-Whitman released a newsletter with a schedule of implementation and action plan as its response to the appeal decision. The exclusion and limits on power boating were not scheduled for implementation in 1996 and it appeared that the Forest Service would delay its limitations on power boat access until 1997. The agency made it clear, however, it intended to move forward with the plan, complete with the power boat exclusion feature and use levels backed down to the 1988-1992 base period.

Supervisor Bob Richmond announced that he would, in response to the appeal decision, further analyze specific effects of his plan on commercial use and issue a new decision on that topic. He would also review his approach to private land access. His team was to begin gathering public comments prior to January 1, 1996.

The newsletter contained a schedule for plan implementation. Here are pertinent excerpts:

Currently in effect:
- a primary use season from the Friday before Memorial Day through September 10
- prohibit personal motorized water craft
- establish no-entry zones where known fall Chinook redds are threatened

By November 15, 1995:
- pack in fuel wood, in compliance with firepan requirements/seasonal fire closures

Legislation: Facts to Justify Regs

- implement a chainsaw closure.

Between November 15, 1995, and May 24, 1996:
- remove navigation markers in the wild river, upstream of Kirkwood Historical Ranch
- remove picnic tables at wild river camps
- remove some structures in the river corridor, such as a metal shed at Pittsburg Landing

Between May 1, 1996 and May 24, 1996:
- require private power boaters and floaters to have approved human solid-waste carryout equipment in their possession prior to entering the wild river corridor
- require commercial power boats to be equipped with onboard (toilets), or approved carryout equipment
- remove pit toilets from the wild river section

Effective May 24, 1996:
- implement a no-wake zone at administrative and developed sites.
- limit maximum private float craft / parties to 8
- establish campsite stay limits
- prohibit camping outside designated sites
- prohibit the launching of inflatable water craft from private power boats in the wild river year-round and in the scenic river on Friday through Sunday, year-round
- eliminate the use of kickers on noncommercial float craft in the wild river year-round

On December 19, 1995, Richmond sent a letter announcing the Proposed Action on the Environmental Assessment (EA) evaluating the economic impacts of the federal environmental impact statement (FEIS) on outfitter operations. A meeting was held on January 24, 1996, to outline the process. Power boat outfitters universally opposed the methodology – an analysis of gross receipts – proposed to determine economic impacts.

Over the next few months the Hells Canyon Alliance proposed an alternative method accessing economic affects, a model which considered indebtedness and profit margin. While initial contacts with the Forest service seemed promising, it soon became evident the agency was proceeding full speed ahead with its gross receipts analysis and had no interest in working out a better method.

As the Alliance was attempting to revise its model to accommodate Forest Service comments and suggestions, they discovered that the forest supervisor had made his decision not to use it a month earlier. At this point, the Alliance withdrew its model to protect those outfitters who had provided sensitive financial information to support it.

On July 17, 1996, the forest supervisor released his environmental assessment for a 30-day comment period. The non-motorized window was still there, expanded to every other week, June through August, excluding the 4th of July. The daily allocations were substituted with a system allocating boat days by the month for larger outfitters and by the season for small outfitters. The boat day allocation for Armacost was increased because of erroneous information used to make the initial allocation.

This was a distinct improvement over the final environmental impact statement, but the allocated launches, particularly in the wild river, were still too low and discretionary launches were largely allocated to mid-sized outfitters at the expense of small and large outfitters. The cutoff point for scenic launches was now Kirkwood Bar, another small improvement. The so-called economic analysis was the look at gross receipts with unsupportable assumptions. It was not an accurate analysis.

The final decision notice was issued September 9, 1996. Again, no changes were made in the economic analysis. In response to requests from commercial floaters the monthly allocation was shifted to bi-weekly and the 4th of July was included in the non-motorized period, now a hard and fast twenty-one days per year. Although over 90% of the comments received asked the Forest Service to drop the non-motorized window, this input was ignored. Comments were summarily disposed of by unsubstantiated comments, such as "we can do it," or "this doesn't apply."

An unprecedented number of appeals were filed, seventy at the final count. A private meeting was held between commercial floaters, Forest Supervisor Richmond and Planning Staff Director Kurt Wiedenmann in early August, well after the comment period had expired on July 19, 1996.

It is evident, from the content of two August 2, 1996, float outfitter letters the HCA had acquired, that a new alternative without the non-motorized window was discussed at the meeting but discarded because of opposition from the floaters. They also objected to excluding the 4th of July from the non-motorized window and requested that the monthly allocations for power boat outfitters be dropped.

The final economic assessment kept the window and complied with most requests. Comments from float outfitters were accepted weeks after the deadline. The Forest Service claimed that no notes were taken at the meeting.

The reaction from the major interest groups as well as others, was damning and immediate. One environmental group and seven commercial floaters sued the Forest Service, challenging the issuance of the stay for the 1995 control season, and attempting to force implementation by June 20, 1995. The lead environmental group (Hells Canyon Preservation Council) opposed power boats in the canyon; its Executive Director Bailey consistently refused any accommodation with power boaters.

The seven float outfitters were big financial winners in the latest Forest Service plan, gaining exclusive commercial access to the heart of Hells Canyon for 41% of the peak use season. Their request for an injunction against the stay was denied.

On January 12, 1996, the Preservation Council again filed suit to force implementation of the management plan in the 1996 boating season, including the power boat limitations postponed by the regional forester until the fall of 1996. In this suit all but two floaters had dropped their support. However, several new organizations had been induced to join into a fray, about which they knew little to nothing.

These included the National Organization for River Sports, Wilderness Watch, Rivers Council of Washington, American White Water Affiliation and Northwest Rafters Association. The suit also asked the court to impose limits on power boaters at the 1975 use level on the wild river and the 1978 use level for the scenic river.

A Portland judge heard the suit but did not grant relief. He instead decided to monitor the Forest Service's progress and left the door open to require implementation if he wasn't satisfied. However, the judge later began to grasp just how contentious the issues were and asked the Hells Canyon Alliance to submit a motion to dismiss.

Forest Service chief Max Peterson, in another unprecedented move, exercised a little known and never before exercised authority to waive the administrative process as a barrier to taking the issues directly to court. The Hells Canyon Alliance's attorneys doubted that this would be considered feasible by the court until the appeals were disposed of and there was a plan to litigate. This move demonstrated just how cemented the decisions were.

To the HCA, there appeared to be no intent by the regional forester to overturn any substantial part of the plan in response to appeals. The HCA subsequently learned that much of the environmental assessment was authored or edited by the regional forester's staff, the very people who responded to the appeals who also did the responding to the severely flawed economic analysis.

Recognizing that it was more and more contending with a stacked deck, the Alliance opted to introduce legislation that would clarify what Congress originally intended. Senate Bill 1374 was introduced by Idaho Senators Dirk Kempthorne and Larry Craig and a companion bill, House Bill 2568, was introduced by Oregon Representative Wes Cooley on November 1, 1995. These measures would, once and for all, settle the issue of shared use by boaters.

The bills were cosponsored by First District Congresswoman Helen Chenoweth of Idaho, and Fifth District Congressman George Nethercutt of Washington. Congressional hearings were held in Idaho and Washington, D.C., and it looked as if passage was possible. However, Cooley soon found himself in trouble over apparently false statements he had made concerning his military service and education.

Cooley was forced to withdraw from the fall election as a candidate. Since this was a major election year, some of the bill's support in the Senate also evaporated, forcing Craig to withdraw it. The bills were reintroduced, with some changes (as outlined below), shortly after Congress convened in January 1997, and subsequently became law.

The alliance did recognize, however, changes were needed in their language: Congress and the original supporters of the Hells Canyon National Recreation Area Act thought it contained language adequate to protect both power and float craft uses. It later became obvious, that the Act's validity provision was not sufficient. The bill introduced November 1, 1995 clarified congressional intent, and confirmed that motorized and non-motorized river craft were to be permitted access to, and use of, the entire river within the recreation area at all times of the year. It established that use was to be allowed at levels not less than those of the past three years, recognized daily and seasonal use patterns. Finally, it provided for access to and from private property in the usual and accustomed manner.

The 1975 Hells Canyon National Recreation Area Act recognized both motorized and non-motorized river craft as valid uses of the Snake River within the recreation area. However, in spite of that, the Forest Service had consistently attempted with each of its management plans to eliminate power boats from a major section of the river for a significant portion of the year. The last plan had slashed private and commercial power boating and threatened to devastate businesses built around this activity.

While the regional forester remanded the plan on appeal to the Wallowa-Whitman's Forest supervisor for further analysis, he left the door open to eliminate motorized craft from part of the river for part of the year; The stage was set for this expensive and divisive battle to go on for the foreseeable future.

With the passage of this simple but effective piece of legislation, the Forest Service and those who love Hells Canyon got on with working together to preserve and protect its marvelous resources.

Legislation: Facts to Justify Regs

Key provisions of the new bill:
- the use of motorized and non-motorized river craft was recognized as a valid and appropriate use of the Snake River within the recreation area;
- motorized and non-motorized river craft were permitted access to, and use of, the entire river within the recreation area at all times during the year;
- concurrent use of the river within the recreation area by motorized and non-motorized river craft would not be considered a "conflict;"
- use of commercial and private motorized and non-motorized river craft was allowed to continue throughout each year at levels that were not less than those occurring in an average of the 3 calendar years preceding the date of enactment, and in daily and seasonal use patterns similar to those experienced in those years;
- personal use of motorized and non-motorized river craft on the Snake River within the recreation area by owners of private property for the purpose of traveling to or from their property.

In February, 1996, the Hells Canyon Alliance proposed a modification to S.B. 1374 and H.B. 2568 that would improve its minimum use level provision. The changes proposed made it more compatible with Forest Service policy and better reflected actual conditions experienced on the river, considering yearly variability. They also made sure the river's managers did not needlessly and vindictively limit growth potential by selecting a measure of use irrelevant to conditions on this river.

Why make these changes? Use of the average of the highest two of the last five year's actual use was the manner in which Forest Service policy called for assignment of outfitter-guide priority use. It was desirable to keep some continuity between the law and established practices for the outfitting industry.

The 5-year period gave a broader base for the calculation of use. Many variables such as unseasonal high and low water flows affected the amounts and patterns of use.

Since Hells Canyon's trout fishery is based on residual steelhead smolts, depending on migration conditions, some years produced excellent trout fishing and others were poor. Fires, weather, salmon smolt flushes and other variables could come into play on any given year, affecting the amount, type and distribution of recreational boating. The five years, 1992 to 1996, included most of these factors and gave a better picture of the canyon's variability than the three years, 1994 to '96. By selecting and averaging the highest two of five years, power boaters were more closely reflecting use levels of the better boating years, the years when boating was most likely a factor in the canyon's social setting, a setting most found satisfactory. In years with poor conditions, such as flooding, drought, smoke from fires and poor fishing; those natural factors effectively limited use without agency intervention.

The Forest Service did not have reliable use figures for private power boating until they purchased the Cache Creek Ranch at the NRA's North Boundary and staffed that portal in 1991. Use estimates prior to 1991 depended on unenforced self-issued permits producing data little better than an educated guess. By basing use on the highest two of the past five years, interest groups were including the entire period for which they had reasonably reliable estimates.

Regulating boating use by launches or boat days, rather than service days, responded to on-river encounters, launch capacity and campsite availability, while allowing some room for growth. If one wanted zero growth because of resource impacts, but not limited by physical considerations such as campsites or launch capacity, service days could work (one person on the river for any part of a day = one service day). This is the manner in which floating is regulated on the Rogue River. Hells Canyon has not yet experienced resource problems that require limits of use for either floating or power boating. The premature USFS decisions to limit power boat use are based on social conditions, the limits of float access were based on physical limitations of the launch site's capacity, and the number of available campsites in the first two day's float. A power boat generates a social encounter on the river that has nothing to do with the number of people on board; the encounter is the same for four or forty occupants.

    This activity was generally regulated by boat days (one boat on the river for any part of one day). The use of boat days allows some increase in the number of people who can experience the canyon if each boat is loaded to its effective capacity. In the past the actual number of passengers in many power boats had been less than capacity. Use can increase within restrictions with no impact on the canyon's social conditions, the limiting factor for power boating.

    Floaters currently are limited on the basis of launches (one party entering the river for a trip of varying duration, ending when the party departs the river). This system has worked quite nicely. Each party progresses down the river, hopefully in a cohesive group of boats. They camp together, each party occupying one campsite regardless of party size. Basing use limitations on launches (or number of parties entering the river) addresses available campsites and launch site capacity, while allowing some room for growth up to the maximum party size each campsite can accommodate. Assignment of campsites would eliminate most of the problems currently encountered by floaters.

The language of S.B. 1374 set a minimum level of use. The Forest Service would not be allowed to regulate use to levels below that minimum. It did not set a maximum, and the agency could allow growth to take place within the canyon's capacity. Some ability to grow is necessary for any healthy business. It is unlikely that the agency will substantially change the launch-based system already in place for commercial float businesses. It has been used for years and is compatible with the bill's language. Float outfitting businesses grew by expanding the actual party size within whatever the Forest Service established as a cap, twenty-four people in the 1994 plan. They have also failed to utilize all of their allocated multi-day launches on some years and have pool launches available. There is room to expand into the current launch allocation.

Power boaters were certain the Forest Service would interpret the minimum level of S.B. 1374 as also being a maximum. The HCA folks cautiously hoped the USFS would be open minded and allow an increase, if it could be accommodated, within the river's capacity. Its past track record, however, pointed towards that being unlikely.

The only way power boat outfitters are assured any growth potential is to fill their craft to capacity; boats sometimes enter the HCNRA with less than a full load. A system of allocation based on boat days or launches allows growth in numbers of passengers within boat capacity for day trips or up to 24 for those rare overnight trips camping on National Forest sites. (Most overnight commercial power boat use is currently based at resort facilities).

Unlike floaters, the power boat outfitters would have no unused launch allocation in which to expand.

Legislation: Facts to Justify Regs

If the agency elected to limit all possibility of increase in power boat business, a purely vindictive measure with neither a resource or social purpose. It could do so by limiting access on the basis of service days. This would lock the number of customer days into the level of the law's formula with no possibility of growth. The same measure would be equally destructive to float businesses. HCA did not want that option to be available. At the end of the day, the Hells Canyon Alliance adopted "Responsible Shared Use" as its operating philosophy. (See Sandra Mitchell's essay in appendix.)

THE FUTURE OF ALMOST HEAVEN

THE LATE JOHN DENVER had a hit song in the late 60s entitled "Almost Heaven." It was a paean to the Blue Ridge Mountains of West Virginia, but as far as westerners are concerned, the Blue Ridges barely qualify as mountains. In their eyes, Denver would have been better off grouping that song with another of his hits – "Rocky Mountain High."

Regardless, those who love Hells Canyon do have a feeling while in the canyon, for whatever reason, that they are almost in heaven. The appropriate word is "ineffable," which means impossible to describe. Another rarely used but appropriate word is "nemophilist," one who loves the beauty and the solitude of the wild. It is hard to put the mystical feeling that grip all but the most obtuse into words. Those who have been seduced by the canyon are passionate in their feelings regarding this special place.

Most canyon aficionados hold strong views about anything and everything having to do with it.

It is too easy to forecast continuing conflicts in perpetuity for Hells Canyon, but incompatible activities, such as clear-cutting old growth timber near trailheads and campgrounds, or attempting to sustain the canyon's herd of bighorn sheep when domestic sheep are still allowed to graze, or removing tables at semi-established camp sites, has environmental groups dismayed.

The fundamental issue, Brock Evans and Ric Bailey argue, is that the Forest Service manages the sacred ground under a mutiple-use philosophy in the manner of the hundreds of ranger districts throughout the national forest system.

Evans and Bailey argue that protection of the resource and recreation in a wilderness setting ought to be the guiding, over-arching management regime. A district ranger should not be worrying about getting out any timber cut or allowing for mineral entry. It is safe to say that as long as the Forest Service manages in this manner there will be pressure from the environmental community to turn management over to the National Park Service.

Another festering sore is the RV Park at Lower Pittsburg Landing the Forest Service rammed down the publics throat. Despite serious questions about placing a 40-unit park with hookups in a spot with no trees and where the temperature can soar to 115 degrees in the summer, the Forest Service plowed ahead.

It built and paved a road to a nearby pristine petroglyph that had stood there for a thousand years. Easy access virtually guaranteed it would be vandalized and within several months it was.

In addition, the road up and over Pittsburg Saddle is steep, particularly on the downhill river side, requiring cars, pick-ups, and RV's descend in first gear or risk a disaster.

While the National Park Service's mission cannot be labeled exclusively single use, it has far fewer requirements than a multiple-use mission. The biggest road block in the beginning was national parks do not permit hunting in the Lower 48 and Hells Canyon has long been a hunting area for deer, elk, bear, cougars and birds. A park designation would have doomed the area ultimately to no protection.

Some have seized on the designation of "park preserves" on the edges of several of the new national parks in Alaska. They believe several park preserves could be created in and around a Hells Canyon National Park.

Some within the renamed Hells Canyon

Conservation Council believe the park battle is over and will not be revisited. Besides, some of these strong Northwest environmentalists are more intrigued by a concept Ric Bailey advocated when he breathed new life into the Council in the mid 90's.

Bailey and others are convinced the future should see the creation of a Hells Canyon/Eagle Cap Wilderness Ecosystem Park. They argue there is an almost unique set of flora and fauna across the northeastern Oregon and west central Idaho landscape that requires smarter management on a larger scale than previously envisioned.

In May 2017, at the annual fundraising dinner in Portland, it rebranded with a new name, the Hells Canyon Conservation Council. The group also announced a full-court press campaign to ensure migratory pathways from Idaho to the mountains in northeast Oregon which all protected by a wilderness designation.

"The HCCC intends to concentrate on ensuring these important animal migratory routes are not destroyed by human greed," Evans states, adding, "we will call it our Connections Campaign."

Supporters of the canyon also recognize that it is nice to have the Park Service club to wave around occasionally when the Forest Service steps too far away from the protection/recreation mandate. While, it may never happen, it will be discussed – and cussed – for many years to come.

If nothing else, the Park Service has a history of doggedly biding its time for years before obtaining a coveted place they believe worthy of protection in perpetuity. Witness in Idaho the recent the rebirth of an effort to turn the Craters of the Moon National Monument into a National Park. Others also argue that the Wallowas should become part of the Nez Perce National Historical Park.

Paul Fritz, long-time supervisor of the Craters of

the Moon National Monument would roll over in his grave were the effort to make Hells Canyon a national park cease.

Conversely, he would rise from the grave if he thought he could influence a decision to jump-start the issue. Fritz was a founding member of the HCPC, but he didn't join it just for altruistic reasons. He wanted the area to be managed by the NPS, and it nearly broke his heart when neither Governor Andrus nor Senator McClure, would support the idea.

Some still believe the Andrus/McClure concern regarding the threat of being "loved to death" if it becomes a national park remains. Others believe that concern has decreased with the passage of time and the relative remoteness of the location.

Mitchell argues passionately there is still no rational basis for banning jet boats above the Jordan Ranch and Kirkwood Bar (The "wild" part of the "wild and scenic" designation on the Snake River from Hells Canyon dam) Mondays, Tuesdays and Wednesdays every other week during the "tourist season" – from early June to mid-September.

Bailey views this "compromise" as a significant victory for those who believe they are entitled to hear no mechanical noise while floating the river. Mitchell still sees it as a sell-out by the Forest Service to the environmental community that disregards the views of those living in close proximity to the canyon.

Fears also remain that another sacrifice of an historical use may be "just around the bend" – the banning of small aircraft in the canyon. There are several historical "back country" dirt airstrips in Hells Canyon that pilots in Piper Cubs, deHaviland Beavers or Cessna 180s and 182s have used over the years. One is on Big Bar on the Idaho side across from Temperance Creek Ranch; another is on the Oregon side across from Pittsburg

The Future of Almost Heaven

Carlson and Richards families rest on the trail while hiking out to Upper Pittsburg Landing.

Landing; a third is adjacent to the Hat Point Lookout on the Oregon side on the canyon rim; and, the fourth is next to Dug Bar on the Oregon side.

Since much of the land along the Snake within the NRA is also classified as wilderness, these landing strips are grandfathered in under the 1964 Wilderness Act sponsored by Senator Church, who understood that if the strips were not explicitly grandfathered the Forest Service might try to close them down.

The protection language is explicit, the backcountry airstrips will be preserved. In an interview, Bailey indicated he personally had no issue the landing strips that were away from the river, but sympathized those who did not like to see or hear planes landing at rivers edge.

Both Evans and Bailey also believe that a national park designation for the canyon would not imperil the current compromise regarding the noise issue.

On the air strip issue, Bailey does make an

exception for the airstrip adjacent to the Hat Point Lookout on the canyon rim on the Oregon side. He described how irritating it was for him one day to witness a small plane doing "touch and goes" for over two hours. This is a festering issue and will be for several years to come. While most don't see this as a problem in search of a solution, others do.

Another point of discord is the Forest Service continued granting of grazing permits for domestic sheep in the canyon. From the beginning of the efforts to protect the canyon, proponents recognized the historical use of sheep grazing had to be grandfathered into any bill. Otherwise, proponents would be up against the then politically influential Idaho Cattleman's Association and the Idaho Woolgrower's Association.

At the time, Governor Andrus and Senator McClure agreed that allowing the historical grazing of domestic sheep was politically prudent.

What no one recognized at the time was that the domestic sheep carried a virus that spread to the canyon's bighorn sheep with devastating results. Indeed, most of the bighorns sheep native to the area were killed off necessitating in the eyes of state and federal fish and game agencies the reintroduction of big horns elsewhere in the Northwest.

This, coupled with a temporary suspension of grazing permits has allowed the big horn to make a comeback.

These unresolved issues could get entwined in a renewed effort to create an even larger national park that would wrap the Hells Canyon NRA into a larger ecosystem that include the Eagle Cap Wilderness. Such a bill would probably include the "connection corridors" the Hells Canyon Conservation Council embraces.

Evans and Bailey, as well as many members of the Hells Canyon Conservation Council, will remain steadfastly committed to getting the NRA turned into a part of the national park system. They believe the Forest Service has prostituted itself with different management plans, all designed to keep multiple uses active, from timber harvesting to hunting to mining.

Evans and Bailey are correct in their assessment that the Forest Service has not been the proper steward the area requires, that their penchant for logging denotes unconscionable support for an extractive use taking precedence over the values associated with a unique resource America should cherish.

APPENDIX

Sunflowers blooming near trail in early April. Photo: Steve Lee

RESPONSIBLE SHARED USE

~ Sandra Mitchell,
Executive Director of the *Hells Canyon Alliance*

Those three words succinctly express the Hells Canyon Alliance's philosophy; a philosophy that emphasizes rights and responsibilities. For example, both motorized and non-motorized craft have a right under the law to use the Wild and Scenic Snake River in the HCNRA but each also has a responsibility to act in a way that minimizes their impact on the resource as well as on the other users. With the rights granted to us in the laws, come responsibilities.

The phrase goes beyond simply advocating multiple use. It requires from those who advocate it a willingness to not be selfish. It means other's preferences are accepted recognizing that one's choice of recreation is not better than another, just different. Behavior is courteous and respectful at all times and is not dependent upon others behavior.

If all recreationists were willing to live "responsible shared use" and not just mouth the words, the conflicts we see over our public lands would for the most part evaporate. Contact would no longer be confused with conflict, encounters would be not viewed as an intrusion upon solitude, and as a result, everybody's experience would be enhanced.

Conflict is a word we hear all too often in human discourse, an integral part of the human condition. We first experience it when we leave the warm confines of our mother's womb to be greeted with a stout slap on our behinds. From then on it is downhill – establishing ownership of toys other children covet with a loud "MINE!" Competing in school, sports and jobs to establish our position in society and protecting our assets are as natural as breathing. When our space, possessions, status or security are challenged we bristle and defend, sometimes with words and sometimes with actions.

But conflict in our lives comes in different degrees and part of belonging to a civilized society requires that we adjust our responses accordingly. Wars such as those in Korea and Vietnam are described as conflicts, human disagreement on a grand scale. As we come down the conflict scale we find political infighting, road rage, crimes of passion, and, somewhere near the bottom in significance to society, just above the childish "MINE", we find disagreements about recreation pursuits.

In managing outdoor recreation and responding to shouts of conflict, managers need to keep things in perspective. There are more and more of us occupying this earth and we are simply going to have to learn to get along. Like the children in a family that can afford only so many toys, we are going to have to learn to share the ones we have. There is real conflict and there is manipulative whining.

In management planning, our public land agencies are constantly assailed with shouts of conflict. Managers themselves often jump on the bandwagon, driven by their own biases or wanting the hero status of a conflict solver. Recreation allocation decisions are usually driven by the desire to alleviate someone's perception of conflict. Those who claim the most conflict, those who are most offended by other users are generally rewarded with restrictions on the other parties who may not have a clue why they are a problem.

Exclusive use leads to regulation, creating a need for strict enforcement and thus creating even more conflict, this time real, with the managing agency in the middle of it. Citizens and taxpayers do not take kindly to being excluded from their public lands unless there is a clear and persuasive reason to do so. When the only reason is to placate the wants of another sector of recreationists their hackles elevate and the level of conflict cranks up several notches. Now the recreationists are polarized against each other and both hate the agency, one for giving away their access and the other for not getting what they wanted.

A good example of this conundrum is the Snake River in the Hells Canyon National Recreation Area. During the LAC collaborative process initiated by the Forest Service to develop a river recreation management plan the idea surfaced to have exclusive use for floaters one week and power boaters the next. It took very little discussion to put that sick puppy to sleep. No one was willing to give up half of his or her boating season. The results would have been disastrous for both floaters and power boaters. Both decided they could get along quite nicely.

Some of the Commercial floaters, however, saw an opportunity to hurt their main competition and continued to complain about power boaters, encouraging their customers to write letters about those evil people who didn't belong on the river. A few radical private floaters joined in and even tried to generate some float-power boat incidents with cameras running to record the results. While the filming stunt failed, the letters and verbal complaints their campaign generated took their toll. The Forest Service decided power boats and float boats were incompatible, discarded the recommendations of the LAC Task Force and eliminated power boats from the heart of the canyon for 21 days each summer, nearly half of the peak season.

The reason given at a press conference announcing the decision to cut power boat access in HELLS Canyon was: "Power boaters don't mind seeing floaters, but some floaters don't like power boats." Power boaters, who make up 80% of the river's visitors, were rewarded for their tolerance and willingness to share by being excluded. The power boaters paid the price for exclusive use, while the floaters, for shouting "CONFLICT" were rewarded with exclusive use. This decision was not in any way driven by resource issues. It was solely based on a desire by the Forest Service to eliminate social conflict. Guess how power boaters feel about the Forest Service and floaters now. Now we have serious conflict on a river where user groups had coexisted successfully for years.

Hells Canyon isn't an isolated case when it comes to rewarding the intolerant minority at the expense of a tolerant majority or trading serious conflict for what were actually minor dislikes and occasional whining. In just about every case where non-motorized users have shouted conflict, they have been rewarded by excluding the folks they don't like. They don't always get everything they want, but they do get a sizable part of it and motorized recreation is squeezed into smaller and smaller areas with every planning effort. On the other hand, the non-motorized folks who raise the issue of conflict never loose anything. By raising conflict as an issue they have everything to gain and nothing to loose. This has in fact, now become a standard strategy for opponents of motorized recreation. Once rewarded in one area, they move to another popular motorized area and begin a campaign of letter writing complaining. Every errant behavior by a motorized recreationist is reported and embellished. Of course every type of recreation has its bad apples and people have lapses in judgment, so there is always fodder for the conflict folks.

In collaboration efforts managers generally address how much public land access motorized recreation should give up and how much should be dedicated to exclusive use by non-motorized recreation. We have give and take on one side and take on the other. One side will give something, it is just a mater of how much; the other side is interested in getting as much as it can. It is impossible to reach a real compromise, because one side can't lose and has no incentive to be reasonable.

The way to level this playing field is obvious; both sides must have something to lose. If non-motorized recreation makes its case for conflict and incompatibility, they should stand an equal chance of losing their access. Managers should give serious consideration to saying, "this is a traditional and important snowmobiling area and you have made a compelling case that there is conflict between you and the snowmobilers. The area is, therefore, closed to non-motorized winter recreation." It wouldn't make many decisions like this to bring a real spirit of compromise to the table.

Decisions driven by real and substantive resource problems are not at question here. Neither are areas such as designated wilderness where motorized recreation is excluded by law. However, many decisions are driven solely by social issues.

There is no question that these decisions must be made, but the present methods by which they are made must change. All citizen owners of the public lands must be treated equitably. When striving for compromise all parties must have an equal chance of winning or losing. The public land agencies must be able to see through any manufactured fog and manage conflict in the context of its real importance to human affairs in the given situation.

THE HEROES OF HELLS CANYON

The Saviors:
Brock Evans, Sierra Club
Sandra Mitchell, Hells Canyon Alliance

Assisting:
Russ Mager, Dick Rivers, Jerry Jayne, Pete Henault, Floyd Harvey, Art Seamans, Doug Scott, Ernie Day, Sanford Stepfer, Dick Wilde, Al McGlinsky, Cyril Slansky, Larry Williams, Tom Davis, Paul Fritz, Cliff Merritt, Art Manley, John Barker, James Campbell, Bruce Bowler, Don Thomas, Morton Brigham, George Hudson, Allen Slickpoo, George Reed, Carmelita Holland, Dick Woodworth, Jack McClaran, Al Klotz, Martin Litton, Frank Craighead, Earl Swanson, Tracy Vallier, Monte Richards, Fred Rabe, Donna Parsons, Max Walker, Walt Blackador, Stacy Gebhards, Lewis Bell, Jack Hemingway, Dick Farman, Schuyler Bradley, Mike Wetherell, Bill Ashworth, Paul Keeton, Jack Bowman, Tony Park, Marty Morash, Russ Mager, A.L. Alford Jr., Robb Brady, Bill Hall, Jim Fisher, Ladd Hamilton, Bill Johnston, Ken Robison, Rick Ripley, John Corlett, Sam Day, Gov. Len B. Jordan, Gov. Cecil D. Andrus, Gov. Robert E. Smylie, Senator Alan Bible, Senator Frank Church, Senator Henry Jackson, Senator Mark Hatfield, Senator Bob Packwood, Senator Mark Hatfield, Rep. Orval Hansen, Rep. Wayne Aspinall, Rep. John Sayler, Rep. Al Ullman, Rep. Edith Green, Rep. Wendell Wyatt, State Rep. Ed Williams, ISU President William E. Davis, Secretary Stuart Udall, Justice William Douglas, Secretary of the Interior Wally Hickel and Elmer Bennett.

ACKNOWLEDGMENTS

There are two individuals whose contributions were critical to bringing this book to fruition and who warrant marquee recognition.

At the top is Brock Evans of the Sierra Club. Gracious with his time, he patiently endured long telephone interviews, follow-up inquiries and provided unlimited access to journals and notebooks written during the effort.

Next to Evans would be Sandra Mitchell of the Hells Canyon Alliance, who also shared time and material with me, providing extensive interviews and refreshingly candid assessments.

To Steve Lee, whose exquisite Hells Canyon photography, such as the photo displayed above, comprises a majority of the photos in *Hells Heroes*, I am extraordinarily grateful. His artistry brought majesty and life to this unique natural wonder.

There were others whose attention, resources and comments were most useful. They include late Idaho Governor and Interior secretary Cecil D. Andrus; his resource assistant and eventual chief of staff, John D. Hough; Gary Catron, former communications director for Senator Len B. Jordan; Andy Brunell, former Andrus resource aide and assistant to the directors of the regional forest offices in Ogden, Missoula and Seattle; Ric Bailey, former Hells Canyon Preservation Council executive director; Mike Wetherall, former chief of staff for Frank Church; John Freemuth, political science professor at Boise State University and executive director of The Andrus Center; Garry Wenske, executive director of the Frank Church Institute at Boise State; AL. "Butch" Alford, editor emeritus at *The Lewiston Tribune*; highly honored photographer Barry Kough, also of The Tribune; late state senator Mike Mitchell of Lewiston; Charles Jones, a member of the HCPC board; and Marina Deborah Waite Ritchie, a member also of the HCPC who generously shared her insightful master's thesis on Hells Canyon written while at the University of Montana in 1988.

I would be negligent if I did not single out two superb staff researchers at the Boise State Library, Jim Duran and Cheryl Ostreider, who were most helpful in assisting me to locate germane material in the Church Archives, the Jordan Archives and the Gracie Pfost Archives.

Grateful mention is due publisher Scott Gipson, president of Caxton Printers, who graciously picked up my manuscript and provided it special attention through publication. His family's publishing business is legendary in the Intermountain West. Additionally, I appreciate long-standing friend and journalist/teacher, Jay Shelledy, who spent many editing hours eliminating redundancies, simplifying sentences and slashing my addiction to

Acknowledgments

employing more words than necessary.

Finally, and most especially, gratitude goes to my incredible spouse Marcia, who is my best editor and sustains me through my health challenges that at times make writing, editing and even reading difficult. Without her loving help, none of this would have been possible.

Chris Carlson
Medimont, Idaho
April 3, 2018

BIBLIOGRAPHY

Andrus, Cecil D. (with Joel Connelly), *Politics: Western Style*, Sasquatch Books, Seattle, 1995.

Ashby, Leroy and Gramer, Rod, *Fighting the Odds: The Life of Frank Church*, WSU Press, Pullman, 1994.

Brooks, Karl, *Public Power/Private Dams*, University of Washington Press, Seattle, 2006.

Caro, Robert, *Master of the Senate*, Vol. IV, Alfred A. Knopf, New York, 2002.

Conley, Cort, *Snake River in Hells Canyon*, BackEddy Books, Boise, Idaho, 1979.

Feldman, Murray, *Idaho Wilderness Considered*, Idaho Humanities Council, Boise, Idaho, 2016.

Hansen, Orval, *Climb the Mountain*, Hansen Press, Boise, Idaho, 2016.

Jones, Jim, *A Little Dam Problem*, Caxton Press, Caldwell, Idaho, 2016.

Jordan, Grace, *Home Below Hells Canyon*, University of Nebraska Press, Lincoln, 1954.

Jordan, Grace, *The Unintentional Senator*, Syms-York, Boise, Idaho, 1972.

Reisner, Marc, *Cadillac Desert*, Penquin Books, New York, 1987.

Ripley, Richard, *Against the Torrents*, BackEddy Press, Boise, Idaho, 2016.

Robison, Ken, *Defending Idaho's Natural History*, KRPress, Boise, Idaho, 2014.

Schwantes, Carlos, *In Mountain Shadows: A History of Idaho*, University of Nebraska Press, Lincoln, 1991.

Smallwood, William, *McClure of Idaho*, Caxton Press, Caldwell, Idaho, 2007.

Wilson, Doris, *Life in Hells Canyon*. CHJ Publishing, Middleton, Idaho, 2002.

Ysursa, Ben, *Idaho Blue Book*, 2013-2014, Caxton Press, Caldwell, Idaho.

Public Documents

Richie, Deborah Waite, *Troubled Waters, Threatened Forests: Hells Canyon National Recreation Area*, thesis for M.A. in Journalism, University of Montana, Missoula, 1988.

Newspapers

Carlson, David Chris, various columns written from Washington, D.C., For *The Lewiston Tribune*, 1971-1972.

Bibliography

Lewiston Morning Tribune

Spokesman-Review

Idaho Falls Post Register

Idaho Statesman

Idaho State Journal

St. Maries Gazette-Record

The Seattle P-I

The Seattle Times

Public Law 94-199, 94th Congress, 12/31/1975

APPENDIX

PUBLIC LAW 94-199—DEC. 31, 1975   89 STAT. 1117

Public Law 94-199
94th Congress

An Act

To establish the Hells Canyon National Recreation Area in the States of Oregon and Idaho, and for other purposes.   Dec. 31, 1975 [S. 322]

Be it enacted by the Senate and House of Representatives of the United States of America in Congress assembled, That (a) to assure that the natural beauty, and historical and archeological values of the Hells Canyon area and the seventy-one-mile segment of the Snake River between Hells Canyon Dam and the Oregon-Washington border, together with portions of certain of its tributaries and adjacent lands, are preserved for this and future generations, and that the recreational and ecologic values and public enjoyment of the area are thereby enhanced, there is hereby established the Hells Canyon National Recreation Area.   Hells Canyon National Recreation Area, Oreg.-Idaho. Establishment. 16 USC 460gg.

(b) The Hells Canyon National Recreation Area (hereinafter referred to as the "recreation area"), which includes the Hells Canyon Wilderness (hereinafter referred to as the "wilderness"), the components of the Wild and Scenic Rivers System designated in section 3 of this Act, and the wilderness study areas designated in subsections 8(d) of this Act, shall comprise the lands and waters generally depicted on the map entitled "Hells Canyon National Recreation Area" dated September 1975, which shall be on file and available for public inspection in the office of the Chief. Forest Service, United States Department of Agriculture. The Secretary of Agriculture (hereinafter referred to as "the Secretary"), shall, as soon as practicable, but no later than eighteen months after the date of enactment of this Act, publish a detailed boundary description of the recreation area, the wilderness study areas designated in subsection 8(d) of this Act, and the wilderness established in section 2 of this Act in the Federal Register.   Publication in Federal Register.

Sec. 2. (a) The lands depicted as the "Hells Canyon Wilderness" on the map referred to in subsection 1(b) of this Act are hereby designated as wilderness.   Hells Canyon Wilderness, designation. 16 USC 460gg-1.

(b) The wilderness designated by this Act shall be administered by the Secretary in accordance with the provisions of this Act or in accordance with the provisions of the Wilderness Act (78 Stat. 890), whichever is the more restrictive, except that any reference in such provisions of the Wilderness Act to the effective date of that Act shall be deemed to be a reference to the effective date of this Act. The provisions of section 9(b) and section 11 of this Act shall apply to the wilderness. The Secretary shall make such boundary revisions to the wilderness as may be necessary due to the exercise of his authority under subsection 3(b) of this Act.   16 USC 1131 note.

Sec. 3. (a) Subsection 3(a) of the Wild and Scenic Rivers Act (82 Stat. 906) is hereby amended by adding at the end thereof the following clauses: 16 USC 1274.

"(11) Rapid River, Idaho.—The segment from the headwaters of the main stem to the national forest boundary and the segment of the West Fork from the wilderness boundary downstream to the confluence with the main stem, as a wild river.

"(12) Snake, Idaho and Oregon.—The segment from Hells Canyon Dam downstream to Pittsburgh Landing, as a wild river; and the segment from Pittsburgh Landing downstream to an eastward extension of the north boundary of section 1, township 5 north, range 47 east, Willamette meridian, as a scenic river.".

(b) The segments of the Snake River and the Rapid River designated as wild or scenic river areas by this Act shall be administered by the Secretary in accordance with the provisions of the Wild and Scenic Rivers Act (82 Stat. 906), as amended, and the Secretary shall establish detailed boundaries of the Snake River segments thereof in accordance with subsection 3(b) of that Act: *Provided*, That the Secretary shall establish a corridor along the segments of the Rapid River and the public lands which would impair the water quality of the Rapid River segment: *Provided further*, That the Secretary is authorized to make such minor boundary revisions in the corridors as he deems necessary for the provision of such facilities as are permitted under the applicable provisions of the Wild and Scenic Rivers Act (82 Stat. 906).

SEC. 4. (a) Notwithstanding any other provision of law, or any authorization heretofore given pursuant to law, the Federal Power Commission may not license the construction of any dam, water conduit, reservoir, powerhouse, transmission line, or other project work under the Federal Power Act (41 Stat. 1063), as amended (16 U.S.C. 791a et seq.), within the recreation area: *Provided*, That the provisions of the Federal Power Act (41 Stat. 1063) shall continue to apply to any project (as defined in such Act), and all of the facilities and improvements required or used in connection with the operation and maintenance of said project, in existence within the recreation area which project is already constructed or under construction on the date of enactment of this Act.

(b) No department or agency of the United States may assist by loan, grant, license, or otherwise the construction of any water resource facility within the recreation area which the Secretary determines would have a direct and adverse effect on the values for which the waters of the area are protected.

SEC. 5. (a) Section 5(a) of the Act of October 2, 1968 (82 Stat. 906), as amended, is further amended by adding the following new paragraph:

"(57) Snake, Washington, Oregon, and Idaho: the segment from an eastward extension of the north boundary of section 1, township 5 north, range 47 east, Willamette meridian, downstream to the town of Asotin, Washington.".

(b) The Asotin Dam, authorized under the provisions of the Flood Control Act of 1962 (76 Stat. 1173), is hereby deauthorized.

SEC. 6. (a) No provision of the Wild and Scenic Rivers Act (82 Stat. 906), nor any of this Act, nor any guidelines, rules, or regulations issued hereunder, shall in any way limit, restrict, or conflict with present and future use of the waters of the Snake River and its tributaries upstream from the boundaries of the Hells Canyon National Recreation Area created hereby, for beneficial uses, whether consumptive or nonconsumptive, now or hereafter existing, including, but not limited to, domestic, municipal, stockwater, irrigation, mining, power, or industrial uses.

(b) No flow requirements of any kind may be imposed on the waters of the Snake River below Hells Canyon Dam under the provisions of the Wild and Scenic Rivers Act (82 Stat. 906), of this Act, or any guidelines, rules, or regulations adopted pursuant thereto.

SEC. 7. Except as otherwise provided in sections 2 and 3 of this Act, and subject to the provisions of section 10 of this Act, the Secretary shall administer the recreation area in accordance with the laws, rules, and regulations applicable to the national forests for public outdoor recreation in a manner compatible with the following objectives:

(1) the maintenance and protection of the free-flowing nature of the rivers within the recreation area;

(2) conservation of scenic, wilderness, cultural, scientific, and other values contributing to the public benefit;

(3) preservation, especially in the area generally known as Hells Canyon, of all features and peculiarities believed to be biologically unique including, but not limited to, rare and endemic plant species, rare combinations of aquatic, terrestrial, and atmospheric habitats, and the rare combinations of outstanding and diverse ecosystems and parts of ecosystems associated therewith;

(4) protection and maintenance of fish and wildlife habitat;

(5) protection of archeological and paleontologic sites and interpretation of these sites for the public benefit and knowledge insofar as it is compatible with protection;

(6) preservation and restoration of historic sites associated with and typifying the economic and social history of the region and the American West; and

(7) such management, utilization, and disposal of natural resources on federally owned lands, including, but not limited to, timber harvesting by selective cutting, mining, and grazing and the continuation of such existing uses and developments as are compatible with the provisions of this Act.

SEC. 8. (a) Within five years from the date of enactment of this Act the Secretary shall develop and submit to the Committees on Interior and Insular Affairs of the United States Senate and House of Representatives a comprehensive management plan for the recreation area which shall provide for a broad range of land uses and recreation opportunities.

(b) In the development of such plan, the Secretary shall consider the historic, archeological, and paleontological resources within the recreation area which offer significant opportunities for anthropological research. The Secretary shall inventory such resources and may recommend such areas as be deems suitable for listing in the National Register of Historic Places. The Secretary's comprehensive plan shall include recommendations for future protection and controlled research use of all such resources.

(c) The Secretary shall, as a part of his comprehensive planning process, conduct a detailed study of the need for, and alternative routes of, scenic roads and other means of transit to and within the recreation area. In conducting such study the Secretary shall consider the alternative for upgrading existing roads and shall, in particular, study the need for and alternative routes of roads or other means of transit providing access to scenic views of and from the Western rim of Hells Canyon.

(d) The Secretary shall review, as to their suitability or nonsuitability for preservation as wilderness, the areas generally depicted on the map referred to in section 1 of this Act as the "Lord Flat-Somers Point Plateau Wilderness Study Area", and the "West Side Reservoir Study Area", and the "Mountain Sheep Wilderness Study Area" and report his findings to the President. The Secretary shall complete his review and the President shall, within five years from the date of enactment of this Act, advise the United States Senate and House of Representatives of his recommendations with respect to the designation of lands within such area as wilderness. In conducting his review the Secretary shall comply with the provisions of section

Public Law 94-199

3(d) of the Wilderness Act and shall give public notice at least sixty days in advance of any hearing or other public meeting concerning the wilderness study area. The Secretary shall administer all Federal lands within the study areas so as not to preclude their possible future designation by the Congress as wilderness. Nothing contained herein shall limit the study areas as part of this recommendation to Congress, the designation as wilderness of any additional area within the recreation area which is predominantly of wilderness value.

(e) In conducting the reviews and preparing the comprehensive management plan required by this section, the Secretary shall provide for full public participation and shall consider the views of all interested agencies, organizations, and individuals including but not limited to, the Nez Perce Tribe of Indians, and the States of Idaho, Oregon, and Washington. The Secretaries or Directors of all Federal departments, agencies, and commissions having a relevant expertise are hereby authorized and directed to cooperate with the Secretary in his review and to make such studies as the Secretary may request on a cost reimbursable basis.

(f) Such activities as are as compatible with the provisions of this Act, but not limited to, timber harvesting by selective cutting, mining, and grazing may continue during development of the comprehensive management plan, at current levels of activity and in areas of such activity at the time of enactment of this Act. Further, in development of the management plan, the Secretary shall give full consideration to continuation of these ongoing activities in their respective areas.

Sec. 9. (a) The Secretary is authorized to acquire such lands or interests in land (including, but not limited to, scenic easements) as he deems necessary to accomplish the purposes of this Act by purchase with donated or appropriated funds with the consent of the owner, donation, or exchange.

(b) The Secretary is further authorized to acquire by purchase with donated or appropriated funds such lands or interests in lands without the consent of the owner only if (1) he deems that all reasonable efforts to acquire such lands or interests therein by negotiation have failed, and (2) the total acreage of all other lands within the recreation area to which he has acquired fee simple title or, lesser interests therein without the consent of the owner is less than 5 per centum of the total acreage which is privately owned within the recreation area on the date of enactment of this Act: *Provided*, That the Secretary may acquire scenic easements in lands without the consent of the owner and without restriction to such 5 per centum limitation: *Provided further*, That the Secretary may only acquire scenic easements in lands without the consent of the owner after the date of publication of the regulations required by section 10 of this Act when he determines that such lands are being used, or are in imminent danger of being used, in a manner incompatible with such regulations.

(c) Any land or interest in land owned by the State of Oregon or any of its political subdivisions may be acquired only by donation. Any land or interest in land owned by the State of Idaho or any of its political subdivisions may be acquired only by donation or exchange.

(d) As used in this Act the term "scenic easement" means the right to control the use of land in order to protect esthetic values for the purposes of this Act, but shall not preclude the continuation of any farming or pastoral use exercised by the owner as of the date of enactment of this Act.

(e) The Secretary shall give prompt and careful consideration to any offer made by a person owning land within the recreation area to sell such land to the United States. The Secretary shall specifically consider any hardship to such person which might result from an undue delay in acquiring his property.

(f) In exercising his authority to acquire property by exchange, the Secretary may accept title to any non-Federal property, or interests therein, located within the recreation area and, notwithstanding any other provision of law, he may convey in exchange therefor any federally owned property within the same State which he classifies as suitable for exchange and which is under his administrative jurisdiction: *Provided*, That the values of the properties so exchanged shall be approximately equal, or if they are not approximately equal, they shall be equalized by the payment of cash to the grantor or to the United States as the circumstances require. In the exercise of his exchange authority, the Secretary may utilize authorities and procedures available to him in connection with exchanges of national forest lands.

(g) Notwithstanding any other provision of law, the Secretary is authorized to acquire mineral interests in lands within the recreation area, with or without the consent of the owner. Upon acquisition of any such interest, the lands and/or minerals covered by such interest are by this Act withdrawn from entry or appropriation under the United States mining laws and from disposition under all laws pertaining to mineral leasing and all amendments thereto.

(h) Notwithstanding any other provision of law, any Federal property located within the recreation area may, with the concurrence of the agency having custody thereof, be transferred without consideration to the administrative jurisdiction of the Secretary for use by him in carrying out the purposes of this Act. Lands acquired by the Secretary or transferred to his administrative jurisdiction within the recreation area shall become parts of the national forest within or adjacent to which they are located.

Sec. 10. The Secretary shall promulgate, and may amend, such rules and regulations as he deems necessary to accomplish the purposes of this Act. Such rules and regulations shall include, but are not limited to—

(a) standards for the use and development of privately owned property within the recreation area, which rules or regulations the Secretary may, to the extent he deems advisable, implement with the authorities delegated to him in section 9 of this Act, and which may differ among the various parcels of land within the recreation area;

(b) standards and guidelines to insure the full protection and preservation of the historic, archeological, and paleontological resources in the recreation area;

(c) provision for the control of the use of motorized and mechanical equipment for transportation over, or alteration of, the surface of any Federal land within the recreation area;

(d) provision for the control of the use and number of motorized and nonmotorized river craft: *Provided*, That the use of such craft is hereby recognized as a valid use of the Snake River within the recreation area; and

(e) standards for such management, utilization, and disposal of natural resources on federally owned lands, including but not limited to, timber harvesting by selective cutting, mining, and grazing and the continuation of such existing uses and developments as are compatible with the provisions of this Act.

SEC. 11. Notwithstanding the provisions of section 4(d)(2) of the Wilderness Act and subject to valid existing rights, all Federal lands located in the recreation area are hereby withdrawn from all forms of location, entry, and patent under the mining laws of the United States, and from disposition under all laws pertaining to mineral leasing and all amendments thereto.

SEC. 12. The Secretary shall permit hunting and fishing on lands and waters under his jurisdiction within the boundaries of the recreation area in accordance with applicable laws of the United States and the States wherein the lands and waters are located except that the Secretary may designate zones where, and establish periods when, no hunting or fishing shall be permitted for reasons for public safety, administration, or public use and enjoyment. Except in emergencies, any regulations of the Secretary pursuant to this section shall be put into effect only after consultation with the appropriate State fish and game department.

SEC. 13. Ranching, grazing, farming, timber harvesting, and the occupation of homes and lands associated therewith, as they exist on the date of enactment of this Act, are recognized as traditional and valid uses of the recreation area.

SEC. 14. Nothing in this Act shall diminish, enlarge, or modify any right of the States of Idaho, Oregon, or any political subdivisions thereof, to exercise civil and criminal jurisdiction within the recreation area or of rights to tax persons, corporations, franchises, or property, including mineral or other interests, in or on lands or waters within the recreation area.

SEC. 15. The Secretary may cooperate with other Federal agencies, with State and local public agencies, and with private individuals and agencies in the development and operation of facilities and services in the area in furtherance of the purposes of this Act, including, but not limited to, restoration and maintenance of the historic setting and background of towns and settlements within the recreation area.

SEC. 16. (a) There is hereby authorized to be appropriated the sum of not more than $10,000,000 for the acquisition of lands and interests in lands within the recreation area.

(b) There is hereby authorized to be appropriated the sum of not more than $10,000,000 for the development of recreation facilities within the recreation area.

(c) There is hereby authorized to be appropriated the sum of not more than $1,500,000 for the inventory, identification, development, and protection of the historic and archaeological sites described in section 5 of this Act.

SEC. 17. If any provision of this Act is declared to be invalid, such declaration shall not affect the validity of any other provision hereof.

Approved December 31, 1975.

LEGISLATIVE HISTORY:

HOUSE REPORT No. 94-607 accompanying H.R. 30 (Comm. on Interior and Insular Affairs).
SENATE REPORT No. 94-153 (Comm. on Interior and Insular Affairs).
CONGRESSIONAL RECORD, Vol. 121 (1975):
June 2, considered and passed Senate.
Nov. 18, considered and passed House, amended, in lieu of H.R. 30.
Dec. 12, Senate concurred in House amendment with amendments.
Dec. 19, House concurred in Senate amendments.

The events of those years can be readily comprehended by presenting them in chronological order:

1954: Four private utility companies, Pacific Power and Light, Portland General Electric, Washington Water Power, and Montana Power and Light incorporate in Oregon under the name: Pacific Northwest Power Company (PNP) to operate and maintain a dam at Pleasant Valley and on the Snake River and apply to the Federal Power Commission (FPC) for a preliminary permit at the site.

1955: The FPC grants PNP a three-year preliminary permit. Five months later, PNP files a construction license application with the Commission for Pleasant Valley and for Low Mountain Sheep – a re-regulating dam 20 miles downstream, just above the mouth of the Imnaha River.

1956: FPC holds hearings on the PNP Co. application. Young Boise attorney Frank Church narrowly wins August Democratic primary by 200 votes over former Senator Glen Taylor. In November, Church, a Democrat defeats incumbent Republican Senator Herman Welker. First District incumbent, Democratic congresswoman Gracie Pfost defeats Republican Louise Shadduck, the first time both major parties have selected a woman to run against another woman for a congressional seat race.

1957: The examiner for the FPC recommends that a license be issued to PNP Company for the project.

1958 : The Federal Power Commission denies the license application (and the examiner's advice) on the grounds that any project which includes the 700 foot Nez Perce Dam, a mile below the mouth of the Salmon River, will make greater use of Snake River hydro-potential than PNP's proposal. Pacific Northwest Power then files a license application for a 670 foot dam (High Mountain Sheep) on the Snake River, a mile above the mouth of the Salmon River.

1960-61: Washington Water Power Power Supply System (WPPSS), a coalition of 18 Washington municipalities, applies to the FPC for a permit to build the Nez Perce Dam under the "public preference" clause of the Federal Power Act. WPPSS also amended its application to include the High Mountain Sheep Dam should the FPC find that project preferable.

1962: Secretary of Interior, Stewart Udall puts the Department of the Interior on record as favoring a *federal* dam at the High Mountain Sheep site. The FPC Examiner issues an opinion in favor of PNP and rejects WPPSS and Interior applications.

1964: The FPC upholds their Examiner's recommendation and issues PNP a 50-year license to build and operate High Mountain Sheep Dam. WPPSS and the Department of the Interior file separate appeals in the U.S. District Court of Appeals for Washington D.C. PNP begins core drilling on the Snake River.

1965: The 9th Circuit Court of Appeals hears oral arguments, re-arguments, and a rehearing.

1966: The appeals court rules 3-0 in favor of the FPC and PNP. Petitions for review filed by WPPSS and Interior are

Timeline

accepted by the U.S. Supreme Court.

1967: The Supreme Court in *Udall v. Federal Power Commission* remands the case to the FPC with instructions to rehear the entire proceedings while considering all issues relevant to "public interest" including "preserving reaches of wild rivers and wilderness areas, the preservation of anadromous fish for commercial and recreational purposes, and the protection of wildlife.) On September 25th the FPC accepts the petition for intervention filed by Brock Evans on behalf of the Sierra Club, the Federation of Western Outdoor Clubs and the Idaho Alpine Club. Russ Mager and members of the Idaho Alpine Club morph themselves into the Hells Canyon Preservation Council (HCPC).

1968: Idaho Senators Frank Church (D) and Len Jordan (R) introduce a bill calling for a 10-year moratorium on Snake River dam building. PNP and WPPSS join forces and file a joint application for the High Mountain Sheep project. Interior Department now seeks federal development of the Appaloosa site, halfway between Pleasant Valley and High Mountain Sheep. Idaho Power completes the construction of the Hells Canyon dam, the third and final of the three dams they placed on the Snake River. The other two are named Brownlee and Oxbow.

1969: The new Secretary of the Interior, former Alaska Governor Walter J. Hickel, announces that Interior has decided to oppose *any* dams on the middle Snake following a float trip in the canyon.

1970: Oregon Senator Bob Packwood and Pennsylvania Congressman John Saylor introduce the HCPC's Snake "National Rivers" bill to Congress. The bill and moratorium die during the session.

1971: The examiner for the FPC recommends issuance of a license for the Pleasant Valley – Mountain Sheep project to the PNP-WPPSS coalition. Idaho Governor Cecil D. Andrus writes the FPC, putting the state of Idaho on record as opposed to further dams in Hells Canyon.

1972: The Senate appropriates $4 million to enable the U.S. Forest Service to purchase private land which is being subdivided in Hells Canyon.

1973: The Hells Canyon National Recreation Area Bill, with backing from Idaho and Oregon senators, is introduced to the U.S. Senate. Field hearings are held on the bill in Idaho and Oregon.

1974: Senate Interior Committee schedules final hearings in Washington, D. C. A two-month delay is caused by the Forest Service announcement that it has no position on the matter and is preparing an alternative plan.

1975: The Senate passes the Hells Canyon bill in June, for the second time. In November, the House approves the bill. President Gerald Ford signs into law the Hells Canyon National Recreational Area Act on November 16th. The Snake River of Hells Canyon has been saved.

CPSIA information can be obtained
at www.ICGtesting.com
Printed in the USA
LVHW02s0906140418
573450LV00007B/9/P